Hatred and Vengeance, My Eternal Portion
(Lines Written During a Fit of Insanity)

Encompass'd with a thousand dangers,
Weary, faint, trembling with a thousand terrors. ...
I ... in a fleshly tomb, am
Buried above ground.

- William Cowper (1731-1800)

Resume

Razors pain you;
Rivers are damp;
Acids stain you;
And drugs cause cramp.
Guns aren't lawful
Nooses give;
Gas smells awful;
You might as well live.

- Dorothy Parker (1893-1967)

I Know a Hundred Ways to Die

I know a hundred ways to die.
I've often thought I'd try one: Lie down beneath a motor truck
Some day when standing by one.

Or throw myself from off a bridge -
Except such things must be
So hard upon the scavengers
And men that clean the sea.

I know some poison I could drink.
I've often thought I'd taste it.
But mother bought it for the sink.
And drinking it would waste it.

- Edna St. Vincent Millay (1892-1950)

Buried Above Ground

Understanding Suicide and the Suicidal Mind

Max Malikow

Buried Above Ground

Copyright © 2017 by Max Malikow

Cover photograph provided by Lois Rader with her permission.

Published by:

Theocentric Publishing Group
1069A Main Street
Chipley, Florida 32428

www.theocentricpublishing.com

Library of Congress Control Number: 2017950880

ISBN 9780998560625

To Rabbi Dr. Earl A. Grollman: my mentor, rabbi, and treasured friend.

To Dr. Glen Jamison: Thank you for your availability when it was needed.

To Dr. Edwin Shneidman: researcher, therapist, author, and pioneer suicidologist.

To Elie Wiesel: Your passing on July 2, 2016 moved me to recall how your sheer decency has made a difference in my life.

Table of Contents

Acknowledgment

I enjoy writing acknowledgments for two reasons. One, they mark the end of a writing project. (I save acknowledgments for last.) Two, they generate gratitude by reminding me the work of writing, which seems solitary, actually is not. Although my interest in suicide preceded this book by at least three decades, the impetus to organize my thoughts on the subject occurred in the fall of 2012 when Dr. Eric Holzwarth, Deputy Director of Syracuse University's Renee Crown Honors Program, encouraged me to propose a course on suicide. His encouragement materialized as PSY 400: Special Topics in Psychology: Understanding Suicide.

In April of 2015, on the eve of his retirement, Eric was properly honored for 30 years of service to the University. It is not an overstatement to say his enthusiasm for my work made this book possible.

Preface

That life is worth living is the most necessary of assumptions, and were it not assumed, the most impossible of conclusions.
- George Santayana

Academically, suicide has been my longtime companion. In 1991 I completed a doctoral dissertation addressing suicide as a psychological, philosophical, and religious issue. In 1999 Rabbi Dr. Earl A. Grollman and I co-authored a book for adolescents who had lost a relative or friend to suicide (*Living When a Young Friend Commits Suicide*). In 2009 I edited a collection of essays about suicide (*Suicidal Thoughts: Essays on Self-Determined Death*). Since 2013 I have taught "Understanding Suicide," a full semester course at Syracuse University.

Moreover, in 1993, at the nadir of my life, I seriously considered bringing an end to myself. I revisited that possibility a few years later when another personal catastrophic event occurred. Undoubtedly these descents into suicide ideation account for the fellowship I have felt and continue feel with suicidal patients. (Since 1987 I have practiced psychotherapy, specializing in the treatment of mood disorders and suicide.) Notwithstanding, I have never encouraged any of my patients to commit suicide. Even in my lowest state, I have sensed the truth of the adage, "suicide is a permanent solution to a temporary problem." (Of course, some problems are permanent, but how they are experienced is temporary.)

Every book should have a specific audience and mission. And like many professors, much of my writing is influenced, if not determined, by the courses I teach. This book was written for students engaged in the study of suicide; students who are seeking to enlarge their understanding of the suicidal mind. Its mission, more easily stated than accomplished, is to contribute to the reduction of suicides. It is ironic that in spite of decades of suicide research and awareness campaigns by organizations like the American Association of Suicidology (founded in 1968), the American Foundation for Suicide

Prevention (founded in 1987), and the National Suicide Prevention Lifeline (founded in 2004) the rate of suicides in this country has remained fairly constant (approximately 12 suicides per 100,000 in the general population). Perhaps the explanation for this irony is the failure of researchers and theorists to effectively convey what they have learned to those who need to know it. Or, perhaps, it is the failure of clinicians to utilize the available information. Yet another possibility is the number of suicides would have increased over the years were it not for the collaboration of researchers, clinicians, and activists.

Realistically, I will be content with the accomplishment of a more modest mission statement: If this book finds its way to a mental health professional or lay counselor and contributes to preventing just one suicide then the time and energy deployed in writing it will have been well spent.

Max Malikow
November 24, 2016
Syracuse, NY

Introduction

The great tragedy of life is not death, but what dies inside of us while we live.

- Norman Cousins

Albert Camus, an existential philosopher, author, and Nobel laureate, wrote: "There is only one serious philosophical problem, and that is suicide" (1953, p. 3). The German philosopher Immanuel Kant posited, "Suicide is not abominable because God prohibits it; God prohibits it because it is abominable" (2016). Another German philosopher, Friedrich Nietzsche, expressed disagreement with Kant with these words: "The thought of suicide is a great comfort: with it a calm passage is to be made across many a bad night" (Evans, 1988, p. 211)

The great thinkers who have written about suicide is no less impressive than the list of noteworthy individuals who have accomplished it. It is a list that includes poets (Hart Crane, Sylvia Plath), novelists (Hunter Thompson, Virginia Wolf), entertainers (Robin Williams, Marilyn Monroe), psychologists (Bruno Bettelheim, Lawrence Kohlberg), Nobel Prize recipients (Percy Bridgeman, Ernest Hemmingway), artists (Alberto Greco, Vincent Van Gogh), and kings (Nero of Rome, Saul of Israel). Sigmund Freud's death was self-determined and Abraham Lincoln struggled with suicidality throughout his adult life.

A few days after Robin Williams' suicide on August 11, 2014 I wrote an unpublished reflective piece:

> A premise of evolutionary psychology is human beings have two fundamental instincts: reproduction and survival. If this is true, it helps us to understand why a suicide is intriguing. Considering the remarkable and sometimes near superhuman things some people have done to survive, it is stunning whenever the survival instinct is overridden by a preference

for death. In the wake of Robin Williams' suicide, I offer five facts:

One, suicide is no respecter of persons. The 40,000 suicides accomplished annually in the United States cut across all demographic distinctions: age, gender, race, profession, income, etc.

Two, suicide correlates with substance abuse. (Note: A correlation is not a cause-and-effect relationship but refers to events or conditions that tend to occur together.)

Three, suicide also correlates with creative genius. The research of Johns Hopkins University psychologist Kay Jamison has established this relationship. It seems the passion that tormented Vincent van Gogh personally also invigorated his work.

Four, suicide is not merely explained by depression. Of course, nearly all suicides are driven by depression. But studies reveal that eighty to ninety percent of people diagnosed with clinical depression do not commit suicide. By analogy, all drowning victims were in water, but not everyone in water drowns.

Five, the suicide of Robin Williams, like that of the brilliant author David Foster Wallace in 2008, is accurately characterized by Shakespeare's Hamlet: "I have that within which passeth show" (Act I, Scene 2).

Regarding Robin Williams' suicide, his autopsy revealed that he had been misdiagnosed with Parkinson's disease. Instead, he had Lewy Body Dementia, an incurable brain disease that causes paranoia, visual hallucinations, motor activity dysfunction, and exacerbates depression. Life expectancy for LBD patients is eight years after diagnosis. His wife described the disease as, "the terrorist inside my husband's brain" and concluded, "however you look at it -

the presence of Lewy bodies took his life" (Schneider-Williams, 2016).

Williams' suicide underscores the necessity of a multidisciplinary approach to the study of suicide. In recent years significant contributions to the field have been made by neurology and genetics (Jamison, 2000, pp. 161-232; Joiner, 2010, pp. 228-236). This treatise includes many of these contributions as well as selected insights from sociology, anthropology, history, and psychiatry. In addition, the pages that follow include psychological, philosophical, and religious thoughts expressed on the subject. Among the questions addressed are: Why do people commit suicide? What is the frequency of suicide? What can be done to prevent it? What help is available to *suicide survivors* in their bereavement? Is suicide a moral issue? How is suicide addressed in the Bible? Why are adolescents especially vulnerable to suicide? Might some suicides be rational?

Engagement in the study of suicide includes exposure to polemics. "Throughout history, suicide has evoked an astonishingly wide range of reactions - bafflement, dismissal, heroic glorification, sympathy, anger, moral or religious condemnation - but it is never uncontroversial" (*Stanford Encyclopedia of Philosophy*, 2004).

I. Epidemiology: How Frequently Does Suicide Occur and What Is Its Distribution?

A single death is a tragedy; a million deaths is a statistic.

- Joseph Stalin

Epidemiology is the study of the frequency and distribution of diseases and health related problems. It is work that is heavily reliant upon statistical analysis, something about which mathematician John Paulos offers a cautionary word:

> Health statistics may be bad for our mental health. Inundated by too many of them, we tend to ignore them completely, to react to them emotionally, to accept them blithely, to disbelieve them close-mindedly, or simply misinterpret their significance (1995, p. 133).

If Paulos' observation is correct, the plentitude of statistics associated with suicide might result in disregard, overreaction, casual indifference, skepticism or misinterpretation. Nevertheless, there can be no meaningful discussion of suicide unless statistics are a part of it. The statistics in this section are from the Centers for Disease Control and Prevention (a government agency) and two research and prevention organizations: the American Association of Suicidology and the American Foundation for Suicide Prevention. These statistics address suicide in the United States. Another cautionary word is provided by Julie Phillips, an Associate Professor of Sociology at Rutgers University who has published research on rising suicide rates: "It's vastly underreported, we know we're not counting all suicides" (Parker-Pope, 2013).

All suicides (2014)

- Number of deaths: 42,773
- Deaths per 100,000 population: 13.4

I. Epidemiology: How Frequently Does Suicide Occur and What Is Its
Distribution

- Cause of death rank: 10

Firearm suicides (2014)

- Number of deaths: 21,334
- Deaths per 100,000 population: 6.7

Suffocation suicides (2014)

- Number of deaths: 11,407
- Deaths per 100,000 population: 3.6

Poisoning Suicides (2014)

- Number of deaths: 6,808
- Deaths per 100,000 population: 2.1

Death Rates for Suicide, 1950–2010

(deaths per 100,000 resident population)

	1950	1960	1970	1980	1990	1995	2000	2001	2002	2003	2004	2005	2010
All ages, age adjusted	13.2	13.2	13.2	13.2	12.5	11.8	10.4	10.7	10.9	10.8	11.0	11.0	12.1
5–14 years	0.2	0.3	0.3	0.4	0.8	0.9	0.7	0.7	0.6	0.6	0.7	0.7	0.7
15–24 years	4.5	5.2	8.8	12.3	13.2	13.0	10.2	9.9	9.9	9.7	10.3	10.0	10.5
15–19 years	2.7	3.6	5.9	8.5	11.1	10.3	8.0	7.9	7.4	7.3	-	-	7.5
20–24 years	6.2	7.1	12.2	16.1	15.1	15.8	12.5	12.0	12.4	12.1	-	-	13.6
25–44 years	11.6	12.2	15.4	15.6	15.2	15.1	13.4	13.8	14.0	13.8	-	-	15.0
25–34 years	9.1	10.0	14.1	16.0	15.2	15.0	12.0	12.8	12.6	12.7	12.7	12.4	14.0
35–44 years	14.3	14.2	16.9	15.4	15.3	15.1	14.5	14.7	15.3	14.9	15.0	14.9	16.0
45–64 years	23.5	22.0	20.6	15.9	15.3	13.9	13.5	14.4	14.9	15.0	16.6	16.5	18.6
45–54 years	20.9	20.7	20.0	15.9	14.8	14.4	14.4	15.2	15.7	15.9	-	-	19.6
55–64 years	26.8	23.7	21.4	15.9	16.0	13.2	12.1	13.1	13.6	13.8	13.8	13.9	17.5
65 years and over	30.0	24.5	20.8	17.6	20.5	17.9	15.2	15.3	15.6	14.6	-	-	14.9
65–74 years	29.6	23.0	20.8	16.9	17.9	15.7	12.5	13.3	13.5	12.7	12.3	12.6	13.7
75–84 years	31.1	27.9	21.2	19.1	24.9	20.6	17.6	17.4	17.7	16.4	16.3	16.9	15.7
85 years and over	28.8	26.0	19.0	19.2	22.2	21.3	19.6	17.5	18.0	16.9	16.4	16.9	17.6
Male, all ages	21.2	20.0	19.8	19.9	21.5	20.3	17.7	18.2	18.4	18.0	18.0	17.7	19.8
Female, all ages	5.6	5.6	7.4	5.7	4.8	4.3	4.0	4.0	4.2	4.2	4.2	4.5	5.0

Sources: Centers for Disease Control and Prevention, National Center
for Health Statistics.

Other Statistics

Of the 7,000 people who die each day in the United States, 117 are deaths by suicide.

On average, a suicide occurs approximately every 12 minutes.

For every accomplished suicide there are 25 attempts.

The annual age-adjusted suicide rate is 12.93 per 100,000 people.

On average, there are 117 suicides each day in the U.S. (Approximately one every 40 minutes.)

Women attempt suicide 3 times more frequently than men.

Men accomplish suicide 3.5 times more frequently than women.

From 1999 - 2010, the suicide rate among Americans ages 35 to 64 rose by nearly 30 percent, to 17.6 deaths per 100,000 people, up from 13.7 percent.

In 2014, Whites accounted for 70 percent of suicides in the U.S.

In 2014, the highest suicide rate by age (19.3 percent) was among people 85 years-old or older.

In 2014, the highest suicide rate by race was among Whites (14.7 percent) followed by Native Americans, including Alaskan Natives (10.9 percent); Hispanics (6.3 percent); and Blacks (5.5 percent).

The suicide rate in the U.S. in 2014 was 13.41 per 100,000. This is the highest recorded rate in the last 30 years.

Though the suicide rate had declined from its previous highest point (a rate of 13.2 in 1980), it has steadily risen since the early 2000's.

The state with the highest suicide rate per 100,000 is Montana (24.5) followed by Alaska (22.7).

The state with the lowest suicide rate per 100,000 is New York (8.6) with the District of Columbia slightly lower (7.9).

Among nations that maintain statistics on suicide frequency the U.S. is in the 33rd percentile. (Evans and Farberow, 1988, p. 79).

II.   Etiology: Why Do People Commit Suicide?

A man devoid of hope and conscious of being so has ceased to belong to the future.

- Albert Camus

Etiology is the study of the cause or causes of a disease or abnormal condition. A reasonable place to begin an etiological study of suicide is to consider if it is an exclusively human behavior.

> In his *Conceptions of Modern Psychiatry*, the American psychiatrist Harry Stack Sullivan stated, "So far as we know, there is nothing remotely approaching (suicide) in the infrahuman primates or any of the lower animals. It is a distinctly human performance." Highlighted on the back cover of Edwin Shneidman's *The Suicidal Mind* is "Suicide is an exclusively human response to extreme psychological pain" (Joiner, 2010, p. 204).

Since "words turn and twist the understanding," the accuracy of these assertions depends on the definition of suicide (Bacon, 2016). If suicide is defined as a deliberate act involving consciousness and intentionality then the instinctual self-destructive acts of animals and insects are not suicidal. This understanding rules out the accidental deaths of lemmings, that seem to leap to their death in the course of chaotic migrations. (These deaths occur when some lemmings fail to survive their plunge over a cliff into the water below.) Fire ants, Malaysian ants, male honeybees, redback spiders, and pea aphids engage in innately driven self-destruction for the purpose of reproduction or colony protection. Psychologist Thomas Joiner had these accidental and instinctual deaths in mind when he wrote:

> Does the death of a severely depressed man, alone in his apartment, by self-inflicted gunshot wound "increase the chance that his genes will persist"? In one sense, of course not.

II. Etiology: Why Do People Commit Suicide?

His reasons involve feeling deeply alienated from others and feeling profoundly burdensome toward others, accompanied by a kind of learned fearlessness of self-injury (2010, p. 216).

Interesting is Joiner's speculation that self-sacrifice might have been adaptive in the course of human evolution but is now "a kind of misfiring of a behavioral module that had adaptive properties in ancestral times but has since become bane" (p. 216).

As previously stated, Albert Camus reduced the study of philosophy to a single question when he wrote, "There is but one truly serious philosophical problem, and that is suicide. Judging whether life is or is not worth living amounts to answering the fundamental question of philosophy" (1955, p. 3). Ludwig van Beethoven's deafness took him to the edge of despair but unambiguously stated that his work prevented him from committing suicide:

> Little kept me back from putting an end to my life. Art alone held me back. Alas, it seems impossible for me to leave the world before I have done all that I feel inclined to do, and thus I drag on this miserable life (Von Andics, 1947, p. 178).

In his fiftieth year the Russian novelist Leo Tolstoy contemplated suicide, asking, "What will come from what I am doing now, and may do tomorrow? What will come from my whole life? ... Is there any meaning in my life which will not be destroyed by the inevitable death awaiting me?" (1929, p. 20). Yet he lived on another 32 years. Perhaps, like Beethoven, his art held him back. But the more likely explanation is Tolstoy's religious experience, described in *What I Believe*, written six years after his personal crisis. In it he rejected organized religion and affirmed his belief in the teachings of Jesus Christ, especially the Sermon on the Mount (Matthew 5-7). Tolstoy characterized his unsought encounter with God with this narrative:

> Yet whilst my intellect was working, something else in me was working too, and kept me from the deed – a consciousness of life, as I may call it, which was like a force that obliged my mind to fix itself in another direction and draw me out of my situation of despair. ... During the whole

course of this year, when I almost unceasingly kept asking myself how to end the business, whether by the rope or by the bullet, during all that time, alongside of all those movements of my ideas and observations, my heart kept languishing with another pining emotion. I can call this by no other name than that of a thirst for God. This craving for God had nothing to do with the movement of my ideas - in fact, it was the direct contrary of that movement - but it came from my heart (James, 1902, p. 153).

Still, knowing why some people do not commit suicide hardly explains why some people do. The testimonies of Beethoven and Tolstoy notwithstanding, many people have committed suicide in spite of their unaccomplished work or relationship with God. The earliest systematic explanation of suicide is found in sociologist Emile Durkheim's *Le Suicide* (1897). In it he classified suicides into four subcategories: *altruistic, egoistic, anomic,* and *fatalistic*, each of which emphasized the individual's relationship to society.

Altruistic suicides occur when individuals choose to sacrifice their lives for the community. The Japanese kamikaze pilots who flew suicide missions in World War II exemplify this type of suicide. Another instance of an altruistic suicide is provided by Kay Redfield-Jamison in her memoir, *An Unquiet Mind*, in which she reflects on her childhood memory of a jet pilot who sacrificed his life for the safety of others:

The noise of the jet had become louder, and I saw the children in my second-grade class suddenly dart their heads upward. The plane was coming in very low, and then it streaked past us, scarcely missing the playground. As we stood there clumped together and absolutely terrified, it flew into the trees and exploded directly in front of us. ...Over the next few days it became clear, from the release of the young pilot's final message to the control tower before he died, that he knew he could save his own life by bailing out. He also knew, however, that by doing so he risked that his unaccompanied plane would fall onto the playground and kill those of us who were there (Jamison, 1995, pp. 12-13).

II.   Etiology: Why Do People Commit Suicide?

Egoistic suicides occur among those who have too few ties to their community. In Stephen King's novella, *Rita Hayworth and Shawshank Redemption*, an elderly convict is paroled after nearly fifty years of incarceration. Released into an unfamiliar world and devoid of relationships, his isolation becomes intolerable and he hangs himself.

Anomic suicides occur when individuals lose their accustomed place in society and cannot adjust to social change. During the Great Depression many unemployed people sank into despair and shame when they could not find work. The suicide rate in the United States increased from 14 to 18 per 100,000 in the 1930's as compared to 10 per 100,000 in 1900 and 1920. A contemporary example of an anomic suicide is that of L'ren Scott, who hanged herself at age 49 in 2014. After a spectacularly successful career as a model and fashion designer, her clothing and accessories company showed a $6 million dollar deficit at the time of her death. Although Wren left no suicide note, it seems she could not adapt to the new life that awaited her on the other side of bankruptcy. One headline reporting her suicide read, "Designer L'Wren Scott was embarrassed and millions in debt when she committed suicide in her Manhattan apartment while devastated lover Mick Jagger was on tour in Australia" (*Daily Mail*, 2014).

Fatalistic suicides result from excessive regulation of an individual's life. A slave or prison inmate might conclude the only way of escape is suicide. Durkheim labeled these suicides fatalistic because they are driven by the perception of being condemned by fate. An historical instance is the anticipation of slavery that occurred in A.D. 72-73 in Israel when the Jewish fortress at Masada was under Roman siege. Rather than being captured and taken as slaves, the surviving soldiers committed suicide, some of them after killing their wives and children (Evans and Farberow, 1988, p. 196). According to the Roman historian Flavius Josephus, when Roman troops entered the fortress they discovered 960 dead and only two women and five children alive (Murphy-O'Connor and Cunliffe, 2008, pp. 378-381).

While this book was being edited former New England Patriots football star Aaron Hernandez committed suicide in a Massachusetts prison. He was serving a life sentence without the possibility of parole for a murder conviction. Reportedly, he left three suicide notes, none of which have been made public. Since his conviction was under appeal at the time of his death, under Massachusetts law he is technically innocent of the murder. The legal principle of *abatement ab initio* maintains if a criminal defendant dies before the completion of the appeals process the case reverts to its status "at the beginning." It has been speculated that Hernandez's technical innocence would require the Patriots to honor his 40 million dollar contract with payment to be made to his four-year-old daughter. If this is the explanation for his death it would mean his suicide is *altruistic*. Another possibility is Hernandez was in despair at the prospect of lifetime imprisonment. If this is why he hanged himself then his suicide is *fatalistic*.

An enigma concerning fatalistic suicides is the low suicide rate among Jews in the Nazi concentration camps. Psychiatrist and Holocaust survivor Viktor Frankl reflected on this in his classic, *Man's Search for Meaning*. He admitted, "The thought of suicide was entertained by nearly everyone" (1984, p. 36). But he added,

> There was little point in committing suicide, for the average inmate, life expectation, calculating objectively and counting all likely chances, was very poor. He could not with any assurance expect to be among the small percentage of men who survived all the selections. The prisoner of Auschwitz, in the first phase of shock, did not fear death. Even the gas chambers lost their horrors for him after the first few days - after all, they spared him the act of committing suicide (p. 37).

In addition to their uninterrupted sense of imminent death, Frankl believed suicide was impeded by their "emotional death," in which despair gave way to apathy. Absence of all emotion, including despair, left them devoid of the feeling that might have motivated their suicide. In David Lester's *Suicide in the Holocaust* the low suicide rate in the camps is addressed as well as the higher than expected suicide rate among survivors years after their liberation (2005). Could it be with liberation came a restoration of emotional life and reacquaintance with despair?

Yet another factor believed to account for the low occurrence of suicide in the camps was the goal of reunification with family. Frankl, who lost his parents, brother, and wife (only his sister survived) stressed the importance of a reason to live. Quoting Friedrich Nietzsche, Frankl wrote:

> ... any attempt to restore a man's inner strength in the camp had first to succeed in showing him some future goal. Nietzsche's words, "He who has a *why* to live for can bear with almost any *how*," could be the guiding motto for all psychotherapeutic and psychohygienic efforts regarding prisoners (p. 97).

Finally, some have speculated that Jews in the concentration camps reasoned if they committed suicide they would be cooperating with the Nazi program that put them there. Hence, they persevered to spite Hitler by inhibiting his plan for their extinction. This explanation, although intellectually appealing, is unlikely because it overestimates the power of vindictiveness to encourage people to prolong their suffering. Chapter IV (Suicide Myths) addresses suicide in the concentration camps as well as its occurrence among Holocaust survivors.

Edwin Shneidman, referred to earlier in this chapter, classified suicidal individuals in a manner similar to that of Durkheim. In *Deaths of Man* (1980) he categorized suicidal people as *death-seekers*, *death-initiators*, *death-darers*, and *death-welcomers*. *Death-seekers* take their lives intentionally and in such a manner that rescue is impossible. *Death-initiators*, often terminally ill patients, refuse life-sustaining procedures. *Death-darers* are those who expose themselves to danger by engagement in high-risk activities. *Death-welcomers* are those who desire to end their life without taking action to effect death and wait for death to arrive in its own time. In summary, death is hastened by an individual's resolve, recalcitrance, foolhardiness or indifference.

Neither Durkheim nor Shneidman provide an analysis of suicide that takes into account the interaction of biological, psychological, and social factors. For a presentation of this approach, the work of several other theorists are considered in the next section.

Theories of Suicide

Concerning the various theories of suicide, the renown thanatologist Rabbi Earl Grollman has written, "It must be stated at the outset that there is no complete agreement even among the great theoriticians. Each scholar and discipline sees the question in a somewhat different light" (1988, p. 26). With this in mind, the following descriptions should not be taken as competing theories since each provides an accurate assessment for a given suicide. Instead, they should be viewed as cooperating theories that collectively address the interacting biological, psychological, and social factors unaddressed by Durkheim.

In "Mourning and Melancholia" (1933), Sigmund Freud fastened upon two drives: the life instinct (*bios*) and death instinct (*thanatos*). He further theorized there is a constant shifting of the balance of power between these competing instincts. Eventually, as individuals age and their quality of life diminishes, death becomes increasingly attractive. Edmund Spenser captured this growing affection for death when he wrote:

Sleep after toil, port after stormy seas,
Ease after war, death after life does greatly please (2016).

Freud denounced murder and suicide as impulsive, destructive actions; characterizing homicide as aggression turned upon another and suicide as "murder in the 180th degree" (1933, p. 220).

David Rudd, past President of the American Association of Suicidology and an expert on combat veteran suicides, has proposed four core beliefs, each of which provides a motivation for suicide.

I am unlovable.
I am helpless.
I am incapable of tolerating my emotional pain.
I am a burden to to others.

A literary example of "unlovability," is found in Edgar Allen Poe's short story, "The Black Cat." The narrator is a self-loathing, tormented soul who first enucleates the eye of his pet cat and then kills it by hanging. The character offers a disturbing explanation of his odious behavior:

II.   Etiology: Why Do People Commit Suicide?

(I) hung it because I knew that it had loved me, and because I felt that it had given me no reason of offence; - hung it because I knew that in so doing I was committing a sin - a deadly sin that would so jeopardize my immortal soul as to place it - if such a thing were possible – even beyond the reach of the Most Merciful and Most Terrible God (2014, p. 11).

The suicide of Lawrence Kohlberg, the eminent psychologist whose research produced the Moral Stages Theory of human development, serves as an example of intolerable emotional pain and burdensomeness. In 1971 he contracted a parasitic infection while doing research in Central America. Eventually his condition deteriorated, recovery was highly unlikely, and pain management ineffective. Facing life as an invalid (intolerable emotional pain and burdensomeness) and in despair (hopelessness), he committed suicide by drowning in Boston Harbor in 1987.

Like Freud, Karl Menninger emphasized the role of the unconscious in self-destruction. An especially interesting feature of his analysis is subintentional suicides in which individuals are unaware of their determination to die. These suicides can take the form of martyrdom, addiction or high-risk behaviors. (High-risk takers are the *death-darers* proposed by Shneidman.) Grollman, in his description of Menninger's analysis, wrote:

The demands of the conscience are so relentless that there is no inner peace. In order to be punished, people often put themselves in circumstances in which they must suffer. They need to atone by being destroyed. A final element is the wish to die. This is illustrated in the impulses of daredevil drivers or mountain climbers who need to expose themselves to constant danger (1988, p. 28).

"Constant danger" is a phrase used by Ernest Shackleton in his call for crewmen to join him in the first expedition to cross Antarctica. Remarkably, more men responded to this posting than the 27 he needed:

Men wanted for a hazardous journey. Small wages. Bitter cold. Long months of complete darkness. Constant danger. Safe return doubtful. Honour and recognition in case of success! (Malikow, 2007, p. 39)

Menninger also gave attention to the meaning of the methods by which people kill themselves:

> In connection with the way in which the need for punishment and the wish to be killed is gratified by suicide we must give some consideration to the significance of the methods used. It is well agreed that, statistically, men appear to prefer shooting and women the taking of poison, gas, or water (drowning). These are obviously related to the masculine and feminine roles in life, i.e. active aggressive and passive receptive (1938, p. 54).

Alfred Adler, a neo-Freudian psychiatrist, believed, "To be a human being is to feel inferior" (2016). Fundamental to his understanding of human motivation is the effort to overcome one's sense of inferiority. But when the individual fails to eradicate this sense of inferiority, suicide becomes the resolution. Those who resort to self-destruction evoke sympathy for themselves and generate guilt for those they leave behind. An example of this type of suicide is found in Olive Ann Burns' bestselling novel, *Cold Sassy Tree* (1984). One of her characters, a cheerless fellow named Campbell Williams, commits suicide after writing this note to his wife, Loma:

> Loma baby, I tried to plan so as not to mess up yr kitchen. i loved you since the day i laid eyes on you jus as pretty now as then. So it ain't you Loma baby its I ain't good for nuthin. which you know. Its got so jus getin out of bed in the morning is to much. I pact up my close and all in a box so you wouldn have to fool with it. My leavin this werl don't have nuthin to do with you bein mad at me for not fixin the fawsit I been aimin to do it a long time fore the fawsit went to leekin.
>   plese save my gold pockit watch for Campbell Junior. i leeve it to him I aired it from my grandedy you know. I love

you an always will but now you can have some pese. tell mr. Blakesly I preshate him givin me the job like he done now he can fine him somebody who can do him a good dase work

i hope god will forgive me so I can meet you in heven. plese don't be mad I have plan it so you wont be the one to fine me.

yr lovin husban Campbell Williams.

p.s. i fix the fawsit

p.s. i wont to be berit in cold sassy so you can vist me some time.

Yr lovin husband Campbell Williams (1984, p. 326).

Elisabeth Kubler-Ross' classic *On Death and Dying* (1969) provided physicians, nurses, psychologists, and hospice workers with the mantra that describes the five stages patients experience when they are told their condition is terminal. (These stages are denial, anger, bargaining, depression, and acceptance.) She addressed suicide by categorizing seriously ill patients who contemplate taking their lives. One category is the patient who has a strong need for control and determines if, "If I can't change that I'm going to die, I can control when and how I will die." These are the patients Shneidman referred to as *death-initiators* who, "break the rules by not taking their medication (and) in that manner ... semipassively promote their own death (Grollman, 1988, p. 34).

Larry Gernsbacher, author of *The Suicide Syndrome*, explained suicide as the culmination of a lengthy self-destructive process.

> ... suicide does not arrive unheralded from out of the blue as an immediate consequence of social conditions or the casualties of life. It arrives as the supreme guest of honor of a comprehensive process unconsciously designed to entertain it (1988, p. 21).

He theorized suicide as the result of the *empirical self* confronting and challenging the *fantastic self.* The *fantastic self* is the misperception of the individual by that individual. The *empirical self* is the real person, the "one who actually exists and actually relates to other people" (p. 38). The suicidal crisis occurs when circumstances exert pressure on the individual to accept the reality of the empirical self and abandon the fantastic, idealized self. Gernsbacher described this potentially fatal confrontation:

> The suicide's unconscious conviction in his Fantastic Self lies at the heart of the Suicide Syndrome. His Fantastic Self is born in fantasy, endowed with fantastic characteristics, and unconsciously experienced by the Suicide as his own true self. His unconscious conviction in it causes him virtually unlimited shame, humiliation, and despair. It underlies all his self-destructiveness. And it alone foments his impending suicide (p. 30).

A character in Victor Hugo's *Les Miserables* exemplifies the Fantastic Self - Empirical Self conflict. Javert, a police inspector who has relentlessly pursued the story's protagonist, Jean Valjean, is a tragic figure owing to his misguided sense of justice. Hugo described him as a man "of two sentiments, simple and good in themselves, but he made them almost evil by his exaggeration of them: respect for authority and hatred of rebellion" (1987, part 4). His obsession with capturing Valjean stems from his binary view of life: there is absolute good and there is absolute evil. Javert was a man who "would have arrested his own father if he escaped from prison and turned in his own mother for breaking parole" and would have done so without hesitation (part 4). His conviction of his self-righteousness and Valjean's villainy is shaken when Valjean extends grace to Javert by sparing his life. Incapable or unwilling to reconsider his view of Valjean or himself, he commits suicide. His torment is captured in the musical version of *Les Miserables* in the song he sings before drowning himself:

I'll escape now from the world
From the world of Jean Valjean.
There is nowhere I can turn
There is no way to go on (Kretzmer, 1986).

Another feature of Gernsbacher's theory is his attention to the "unique combination of assets that distinguish (sic) human beings from other animals: those that go into making human beings human" (p. 27). Each of these assets carries with it a seed that can germinate and grow into a contributor to suicide. Human beings have the ability to imagine, but this can result in envisioning a grim, hopeless future. There is the ability to feel, but this includes agony as well euphoria. The unique human ability to grapple with the meaning of life can indeed make life more worth living. But it can also have the effect of driving a person to the conclusion that life is meaningless and, therefore, not worth living. Absurdity, the belief that life has no meaning, was addressed by Camus in his noteworthy essay, "The Myth of Sisyphus." In it he wrote: "The subject of this essay is precisely this relationship between the absurd and suicide, the exact degree to which suicide is a solution to the absurd" (1955, p. 5). Finally, human beings can conceptualize their death, which can motivate attentiveness in time management, as Viktor Frankl recommended (1959, pp. 161-162). But it can have the opposite effect of imagining a peaceful nonexistence. (It should be noted that Freud believed it is impossible to conceptualize death since an existing being cannot imagine nonexistence.)

When David Foster Wallace committed suicide in 2008 at age 46 it ended the career of one of America's great contemporary writers. His death marked his surrender to the depression that had plagued him since adolescence. An esteemed author, admired professor, and beloved husband and son, his depression could not be attributed to his life circumstances. Rather, his was an endogenous depression, its origin located in his unfortunate neurochemistry.

Another accomplished writer, William Styron, lived a life punctuated by downward spirals into deep depression and suicide ideation. Like Wallace, his depression was endogenous. Unlike Wallace, he lived out his natural life, dying in 2001 at age 81. His memoir, *Darkness Visible* (1990) is a valuable contribution to the literature of psychopathology.

Wallace and Styron are high profile instantiations of biologically driven depression and suicidality. Although Styron did not take his life, he considered doing so innumerable times. Kay Redfield-Jamison, referred to earlier in this chapter, whose bipolar disorder once drove her to attempting suicide, is another instance of a biologically driven mental illness. She has speculated on the existence of a suicide gene, as yet undiscovered. Her record of achievement as a researcher and writer on the subject of suicide combined with recent advances in brain science give credibility to the possibility that some suicides are genetically driven.

III. Suicide and Resilience: Why Do Some People Heroically Persevere and Others Opt Out of Life?

Was mich nicht umbringt, macht mich starker.
(That which does not kill me, makes me stronger.)
- Friedrich Nietzsche

Although the world is full of suffering, it is also full of overcoming it
- Helen Keller

A 1981 *Sports Illustrated* story written by Frank Deford entitled "Kenny, Dying Young" recounts the story of Kenny Wright, a high school football star who committed suicide after a spinal cord injury left him a quadriplegic (Deford, 1981). Three years earlier another football star, Darryl Stingley of the New England Patriots, sustained a spinal cord injury in a pre-season game that left him a quadriplegic. Stingley did not commit suicide. Instead, he finished his college degree, continued parenting three sons, worked in the front office of the Patriots, and started a not-for-profit organization for at-risk youths in his hometown Chicago. Five years after his injury, he wrote a memoir, *Happy to Be Alive* (1983).

Another magazine story, "A Deadly Struggle Against the Sea," describes Janet Culver's fourteen day battle to survive after a sailboating accident (Culver, 1989). Adrift on a life raft with her sailing partner, Nicholas Abbot, on the tenth day he withdrew from the struggle to survive by drowning himself. Janet Culver survived to tell her story.

What accounts for Darryl Stingley's resilience and Kenny Wright's suicide? What enabled Janet Culver to persevere in the same situation that drove Nicholas Abbot to despair and self-determined death? In the preface to a collection of essays on suicide published a few years ago, the editor expressed his long running curiosity about why people commit suicide:

III.	Suicide and Resilience: Why Do Some People Heroically Persevere and Others Opt Out of Life?

> A wise and helpful professor once advised me to locate the "fire that burns within" for the topic of my doctoral dissertation. He reasoned that since I would be immersed in the topic for several years, it should be one that would sustain my interest. I opted for suicide and, fifteen years after the completion of my dissertation, I confess to giving disproportionate attention to suicide in the courses I teach as well as gravitating toward suicidal patients in my clinical work. Why? Perhaps Camus is right: "There is but one truly serious philosophical problem, and that is suicide. Judging whether life is or is not worth living amounts to answering the fundamental question of philosophy" (Malikow, 2009, p. xi).

Why are some people extraordinarily persistent and why do other people opt out of life? As with so many questions concerning human behavior, the variables of personality and perception preclude an uncomplicated answer. Persistence is the quality of continuing in a course of action in spite of discouragement, opposition, and/or failure. Perseverance, the determination to remain constant in purpose, is synonymous with persistence. Resilience, the capacity to return to a previous condition or regain a high level of functioning following a loss, is an expression of persistence. Consider the descriptions of two men and guess which one persevered in life and which one committed suicide:

> In 1973 D.C. was severely burned in an automobile explosion. In the accident he lost two-thirds of his skin, both hands, both eyes, and both ears. In addition to disfigurement, D.C. was facing a lifetime of medical procedures and intense, unremitting pain.

> D.W. wrote a novel that was included on *Time* magazine's list of the "100 Best Novels" written between 1923 and 2003. A brilliant, popular college professor and multiple award winning author, as a teenager he was a nationally ranked junior tennis player.

Given the context of these descriptions, likely you chose D.W. as the one who committed suicide and D.C. as the one who persevered. If you did, you chose correctly. However, even if you guessed correctly, didn't it seem counter-intuitive? D.C. is Dax Cowart, who wanted to die following his accident and for a time appealed to have his medical treatment discontinued. Yet, eventually, he accepted his lot as "The Man Sentenced to Life," graduated from law school, and married (Wicker, 1989). His legal specialty is medical ethics and patients' rights. D.W. is David Foster Wallace, whose suicide in 2008 at the age of 46 deprived the literary world of an extraordinary talent. Wallace had long suffered with a depression that eventually resisted treatment that included psychotherapy, antidepressant medications, and ECT (electroconvulsive therapy). A complete understanding of Cowart's resilience and Wallace's suicide is an impossibility. Nevertheless, from an analysis of a number of instances of people who have persevered and those who did not, a partial understanding is attainable.

Examples of Perseverance

H. Jackson Brown, author of the bestseller, *Life's Little Instruction Book*, has provided a picturesque description of perseverance: "In the confrontation between the stream and the rock, the stream always wins – not through strength but by perseverance" (2012). Albert Camus discovered his own resilience and described it with these words: "In the midst of winter, I finally learned there was in me an invincible summer" (2011). Impressive instances of perseverance and resilience are not difficult to find. Here are a few:

Paul Wittgenstien resumed his career as a concert pianist *after* having his right arm amputated during World War I.

Ludwig van Beethoven began to lose his hearing at age 26 and was totally deaf by age 44, resulting in a career change from pianist to composer.

Elyn Saks is a professor at the University of Southern California School of Law and on the psychiatry faculty of the University of California School of Medicine. She graduated valedictorian from Vanderbilt University, studied at Oxford, and earned her law degree at Yale University. Her bestselling memoir, *The Center Cannot Hold: My Journey Through Madness*, recounts her life with schizophrenia, the condition that manifested when she was eight years-old.

Michael J. Fox has continued his distinguished acting career after being diagnosed with Parkinson's disease at age thirty. He is the founder of a foundation for Parkinson's research.

Examples of Surrender

Also easily found are instances of giving up when challenged. In November of 1980 the phrase "No mas!" was immortalized in boxing history when one of the sport's greatest champions, Roberto Duran, quit in the eighth round of a fight with Sugar Ray Leonard. ("No mas" is Spanish, translated as, "no more.") Far more serious than withdrawing from a boxing match is deciding "no mas" to life as did Kenny Wright and Nicholas Abbot.

Redfield-Jamison's investigation of the occurrence of mood disorders among artistic geniuses generated an impressive list of celebrated artists who chose to end their lives. Poets Sylvia Plath and Anne Sexton, novelists Virginia Woolf, Hunter Thompson, and Lucy Maude Montgomery, and painters Vincent van Gogh and Alberto Greco are among the creative artists who committed suicide. Redfield-Jamison, an accomplished writer herself, once attempted suicide when suffering extreme depression from bipolar disorder. In *Touched with Fire: Manic-Depressive Illness and the Artistic Temperament* she presents the case for, " ... the importance of moods in igniting thought, changing perceptions, creating chaos, forcing order upon that chaos, and enabling transformation" (1996, p. 6). In her estimation, the wide ranging, intense moods that fuel creativity also induce suicidality. Similarly, Sheidman's research revealed an overrepresentation of suicide among people with I.Q.'s in the genius category (1998). Such findings are consistent with the biblical observation, "With much wisdom comes much sorrow; the more knowledge, the more grief" (Ecclesiastes 1:18).

A shocking instance of giving up on life was reported in a *Newsweek* magazine story concerning veterans of the wars in Afghanistan and Iraq:

> About 18 veterans kill themselves each day. Thousands from the current wars have already done so. In fact, the number of U.S. soldiers who have died by their own hand is now estimated to be greater than the number (6,460) who have died in combat in Afghanistan and Iraq (Swofford, 2012, pp. 29-30).

Towards an Understanding

How is the difference in resilience between Darryl Stingley and Kenny Wright explained or the difference in persistence between Janet Culver and Nicholas Abbot understood? A comprehensive accounting for these differences is impossible because all the factors that contribute to an individual's traits cannot be known. *Personality* is the aggregate of those traits; it is "an individual's characteristic pattern of thinking, feeling, and acting" (Myers, 2007, p. 598). The contributions of nature and nurture and their interaction with a continuously changing environment forbid a complete explanation of why some people are more persistent than others. Nevertheless, this does not preclude a moderate understanding towards that end, two conditions that develop persistence will be considered, followed by three contributors to succumbing.

Understanding Persistence

Shortly after graduating from college, Francesco Clark dived into a swimming pool and suffered a spinal cord injury that left him a quadriplegic. In addition to the loss of the use of his arms and legs, he lost the ability to perspire, causing an extremely irritating skin condition. Without formal training in either chemistry or dermatology, Clark developed a lotion to treat his condition. Eventually, this led to the founding of Clark's Botanicals, an international producer and distributor of cosmetic products.

III.   Suicide and Resilience: Why Do Some People Heroically Persevere
and Others Opt Out of Life?

Richard Cohen is a nationally syndicated columnist and four time Pulitzer Prize recipient. In addition, he is nearly blind, twice a cancer survivor, and limited by multiple sclerosis. In his memoir, *Blindsided: Living a Life Above Illness - A Reluctant Memoir*, he shares a daily conversation he has with himself, lest he despair over his continually deteriorating body:

> I feel weak because I acknowledge the realities of my life. We exist in a culture that celebrates strength. Men are strong and self-reliant. I am weakened and need the help of others. There is no escape from the rust I see on my body.
>
> I must rise above the culture of perfection and remember that I can be even if I can no longer *do*. I am learning to acknowledge weakness, accept assistance, and discover new forms of self-definition. My formula has changed. I do not read self-absorbed men's magazines or go to Vin Diesel movies. A new male idea will have to do. I cannot allow myself to be held captive by old dreams.
>
> Success comes today by a different standard, measured by more cerebral achievements and often centered on the lives of my children. ... Dealing with challenges to health is a great ally in nurturing that change in priorities (2004, p. 22).

What accounts for the resilience of Francesco Clark and perseverance of Richard Cohen? One factor is their ability and willingness to reframe their circumstances without denying reality. By constructing different, but nonetheless accurate, descriptions of their situations they have been able to redirect themselves and adapt. Rather than lamenting the loss of their well-functioning bodies, Clark and Cohen have redefined their lives by choosing to focus on new priorities. For Clark this meant abandoning his dream of a career in the fashion magazine industry; for Cohen it meant redirecting the importance once placed on physical fitness (jogging and tennis) toward family and writing. *Framing* is the psychological term for what these men are accomplishing.

> Although it is not a part of clinical jargon, framing is an essential concept in psychotherapy, referring to *how we*

choose to describe a situation. Framing refers to how we feel about and understand our circumstances and largely determines whether or not we will find a reason to be grateful, regardless of the conditions in which we find ourselves (Malikow, 2010, p. 61).

In addition to the capacity to reframe, resilience is strengthened by a sense of responsibility. Nietzsche wrote, "He who has a why to live for can bear with almost any how" (Frankl, 1959, p. 97).

A stunning confession by Abraham Lincoln made it clear that he suffered from nearly unbearable psychic pain:

> I am the most miserable man living. If what I feel were equally distributed to the whole human family, there would not be one cheerful face on earth. Whether I shall ever be better, I cannot tell; I awfully forebode I shall not. To remain as I am is impossible; I must die or be better, it appears to me (Shenk , 2005, p. 56).

Lincoln triumphed over his depression by not allowing it to prevent him from doing his duty. He believed, "he had been charged with so vast and sacred a trust that he felt he had no moral right to shrink from his responsibilities" (p. 66).

> Although Lincoln's theology is not altogether clear, there is no mistaking that he carried on his work with a sense of calling; a determination to accomplish something while he lived; and to have his name connected "with the great events of his generation" (Malikow, 2008, p. 9).

Although few of us will have our names connected with the great events of our generation, we need the reassurance that our life has significance. "We need to know that we matter to the world, that the world takes us seriously" (Kushner, 2001, p. 5).

Understanding Suicide

Recall David Rudd's four central themes in a suicidal belief system. According to his analysis, people who give up on life perceive themselves as unworthy to live, incapable of managing their problems, unable to continue suffering, and diluting the quality of life for others. Rudd's four themes are illustrated by the suicides cited earlier in this book. Janet Culver described Nicholas Abbot as overwhelmed by guilt for his failure to adequately equip the sailboat for an emergency. Unable to forgive himself, he felt he didn't deserve to live. Lawrence Kohlberg was in despair over his helplessness to improve his irreversible condition. In spite of his brilliance, David Foster Wallace was unable to find a way to relieve his psychache. And Kenny Wright concluded he would be a lifelong burden to his devoted mother.

Psychiatrist John Maltsberger has offered two additional themes in a suicidal belief system: rage and aloneness. Rage seems the best explanation for a shocking murder-suicide that occurred in Florida several years ago:

> On May 27, 2006 an Illinois physician threw his eight and four year-old sons from the fifteenth floor balcony of the hotel where they were vacationing. Dr. Edward Van Dyk then followed his sons over the railing by jumping to his own death (Malikow, 2008, p. 85).

Dr. Van Dyk did not leave a suicide note, making it more difficult to explain this tragedy. It is likely this hideous act was motivated by rage toward his wife, for something she actually did or he imagined she did.

In the *Nicomachean Ethics*, Aristotle reflects on the value of friendship: "Without friends, no one would choose to live though he had all other goods" (1999, VIII, p. 119). Few have held on as remarkably and resolutely as Bob Shumaker, held as a prisoner of war for eight years in North Vietnam including three years in solitary confinement. Reflecting on those years, he attributes his survival and resumption of a normal life to the support of his fellow POW's and mental discipline. No doubt the latter was nurtured by his training as a Navy officer and pilot. In an interview Shumaker offered this explanation.

The worst thing I and my fellow POW's could have done under the circumstances would have been to clam up and withdraw. That would have been easy because our captors kept us in four by nine concrete windowless cells; they imposed a no communication policy on us. But we thwarted them by developing a tap code, which allowed us to clandestinely communicate with our neighbors a foot away through a concrete wall using coded knocks that spelled out words.

What did we talk about? It didn't really matter. We just knew that there was a fellow American sharing our experience. We built houses in our minds, tapped out French and music lessons, computed the 12th root of the number two, relived pleasant past relationships and even had elaborate breakfasts each Sunday (all in our imaginations). We were focused on supporting each other, trying to make life a bit more bearable, and dreaming (2010).

Today Shumaker lives in the house he mentally constructed board by board, nail by nail as a POW. (Of course, it has an open floor plan, plenty of windows, and minimal concrete.)

Resiliency also is required of those whose functioning has been impaired by disease or accident. Dennis Charney of the Mount Sinai School of Medicine believes, "Social support is essential to resilience" (2010). Occupational therapists work with patients to assist them in recovering daily living and work skills. Nancy Kelly, Supervisor of Occupational Therapy at Brigham and Women's Hospital in Boston, stresses the contribution of support to a patient's determination to survive and regain as much functionality as possible (2012). A family's love and encouragement combined with professional instruction on how to adapt to life following a spinal cord injury, stroke, amputation, or other misfortune expedites and augments resilience.

Conclusion

Lance Armstrong, a seven time Tour de France bicycle race winner and a cancer survivor, expressed his philosophy of pain and perseverance in his memoir:

> Pain is temporary. It may last a minute, or an hour, or a day, or a year, but eventually it will subside and something else will take its place. If I quit, however, it lasts forever. That surrender, even the smallest act of giving up, stays with me. So when I feel like quitting, I ask myself, which would I rather live with? ...By now you've figured out I'm into pain. Why? Because it's self-revelatory, that's why. There is a point in every race when a rider encounters his real opponent and understands that it's himself. In my most painful moments on the bike, I am at my most curious, and I wonder each and every time how I will respond. Will I discover my innermost weakness, or will I seek out my innermost strength? It's an open-ended question whether or not I will be able to finish the race. You might say pain is my chosen way of exploring the human heart (2000, pp. 269-270).

What is the explanation for Armstrong's determination and pain tolerance? Why isn't everyone like him? Why are some people extraordinarily persistent? Apart from the genetic contribution to personality, a person's training, support, and models provide a partial answer to these questions. Armstrong is reminiscent of a description found in Rudyard Kipling's classic poem "If."

> If you can force your heart and nerve and sinew
> To serve your turn long after they are gone
> And so hold on when there is nothing left in you
> Except the will which says to them "hold on"
> (1910).

Child psychiatrist Robert Coles agrees with the adage, "Values are not taught, they are caught." His five decades of research on the moral development of children has brought him to this conclusion:

> "Moral intelligence" isn't acquired only by the memorization of rules and regulations, by dint of abstract classroom

discussion or kitchen compliance. We grow morally as a consequence of learning how to be with others, how to behave in this world, a learning prompted by taking to heart what we have seen and heard. The child is a witness; the child is an ever-attentive witness of grown-up morality – or lack thereof; the child looks and looks for cues as to how one ought to behave, and finds them galore as we parents and teachers go about our lives, making choices, addressing people, showing in action our rock-bottom assumptions, desires, and values, and thereby telling those young observers much more than we may realize (1998, p. 5).

Coles, Daniel Goleman, William Kirk Kilpatrick, Richard Lavoie, Thomas Lickona and Samuel Oliner, all authorities on moral development and character education, agree the acquisition of values begins in childhood by direct observation. The values children internalize and carry into adulthood are the values their parents and significant other adults have consistently demonstrated. Among these values are resilience and perseverance.

In addition to living out these values, Kilpatrick recommends reinforcing them by reading. He believes character building books are better gifts than clothes or toys. "The clothes and toys won't last and won't make a lasting difference. But what a child reads becomes a permanent part of his life, giving direction to his imagination and actions" (1992, p. 269). Quoting another author, Kilpatrick encourages exposing children to these books and stories even before they are able to read:

I read because *my* father read to *me*. And because he'd read to me, when my time came I knew intuitively there is a torch that is supposed to be passed from one generation to the next. And through countless nights of reading I began to realize that when enough of the torchbearers - parents and teachers - stop passing the torches, a culture begins to die (Trelease, 1985, p. xv).

III.   Suicide and Resilience: Why Do Some People Heroically Persevere and Others Opt Out of Life?

Resilience and perseverance cannot be gift wrapped and given to children as presents. These traits are nurtured by example and reinforced by character building literature.

IV. Suicide Myths: What Are Some Common Misconceptions About Suicide?

It ain't what you don't know that gets you into trouble. It's what you know for sure that just ain't so.

- Mark Twain

Concerning the importance of dispelling widely held misconceptions about suicide, Professor Thomas Joiner has written:

> Like any dangerous and lethal thing that causes human suffering, suicide needs to be understood so as to manage and ally its fearsomeness – survivors deserve this understanding (not to mention compassion). So do those who have died by suicide; we honor them by understanding and combating their cause of death. Dispelling myths and misunderstandings about suicide seems to me a good place to start (2010, p. 11).

Intuitively, a low occurrence of suicide among survivors of traumatic events is expected. It is reasonable to assume that people who survived when survival was unlikely would gratefully live out the rest of their life. But this is not the case for either Titanic or Holocaust survivors. Of the 710 Titanic survivors, eight eventually committed suicide - a ratio of one per 88 survivors. While it is impossible to connect each of these suicides to the sinking of the Titanic, this ratio is a frequency 100 times greater than the general poulation.

Suicide statistics for Holocaust survivors are less precise, but research and anecdotes indicate a high occurrence of suicide among them. Chapter II of this book includes speculation concerning the low occurrence of suicide in the concentration camps. However, Tel Aviv University Professor Yoram Barak maintains the belief there were few suicides among camp inmates is a myth. He supports his position by citing studies that place the suicide rate in the concentration camps at approximately 25,000 per 100,000 inmates. Referring to this statistic in a 2005 interview he said, "As far as is known, this is the highest suicide rate in human history. We've learned that religious people in Auschwitz and other camps made formal applications to rabbis in the camps seeking permission to commit suicide" (Traubmann, 2005).

Regarding the occurrence of suicide among Holocaust survivors. For many years it was believed that survivors rarely killed themselves after liberation. According to Barak this too is a myth. He traced its origin to a 1947 lecture given by Aharon Persikovitz, a survivor of Dachau. Speaking at a symposium of psychiatrists, Persikovitz said, "Holocaust survivors do not commit suicide; they heroically prove the continuity of the Jewish people" (2005). In fact, a study published in 2007 found that 24 percent of Holocaust survivor patients at the Abarbanel Mental Health Center in Bat Yam, Israel had attempted suicide, compared to 8.2 percent of patients who were not survivors (Barak, 2007).   Although Barak has demonstrated Persikovitz's assertion is mythical, he understands its appeal:

> (T)his statement was never checked and is not based on anything. For sociological reasons, it was convenient for all of us to adhere to it. No one wanted to think that Holocaust survivors were in unbearable stress. The survivors themselves also did not want to be stigmatized as "sick, weak, and broken" ... It was convenient to think: "Let's show the Nazis that we're heroes, we established a state" (2005).

Three well-known Holocaust survivors who committed suicide in their later years are the controversial psychoanalyst Bruno Bettelheim and authors Jean Amery and Primo Levi. Interesting is that Amery reflected at length on suicide in a collection of essays titled *On Suicide: A Discourse on Voluntary Death* (1999). In its preface he wrote:

> This text is situated beyond psychology and sociology. It begins where scientific suicidology leaves off. Instead of viewing voluntary death from the outside, the world of the living and surviving, I have tried to view it from the interior of those who call themselves suicidal or suicides. ... What may

appear to be an apologetic (for suicide) is only my reaction to a kind of research that pursues the subject of suicide without being acquainted with the specific human beings in search of their own freely chosen death - who find themselves in an absurd and paradoxical situation (1999, pp. xxiii - xxv).

Responding to Levi's suicide, Elie Wiesel wrote, "Primo Levi died at Auschwitz forty years later" (1987, p. 3).

The balance of this chapter presents the most frequently encountered myths about suicide. The sources of this compilation are *Myths About Suicide* (2010) by Thomas Joiner, *Too Young to Die* (1976) by Francine Klagsbrun, *Making Sense of Suicide* (1997) by Richard Lester, and "Suicide Myths" (2016), an essay by Kevin Caruso, Executive Director of Suicide.org. Each myth is accompanied by a brief commentary countering the myth.

Myth: Suicide is an easy escape - a cowardly act.
Counter: This statement is an overgeneralization. Some suicides are altruistic acts of courage. Other suicides are fatalistic, intended to avert unnecessary suffering when death is inevitable and/or imminent.

Myth: Suicide is an act of anger, aggression or revenge.
Counter: True, suicide is murder and, hence, a violent act. While it is true that some suicides are expressions of anger, aggression or revenge, it is not true of all suicides. The assertion that all suicides are acts of anger, aggression or revenge is another overgeneralization.

Myth: The explanation for suicide is uncomplicated - it is depression.
Counter: Of course, depression is a factor in most suicides. However, not everyone who is depressed commits suicide. In fact, studies have shown that 85 to 90 percent of people diagnosed with clinical depression do not commit suicide. A difference between depressed people who commit suicide and those who do not is the former descend to a state of despair. This being said, not everyone in despair commits suicide.

Myth: People who commit suicide do not make future plans.

IV. Suicide Myths: What Are Some Common Misconceptions About Suicide?

Counter: People contemplating suicide are ambivalent about ending their life. Making future plans is an expression of the part of them that wants to live. Future plans might provide a reason for them to continue living. The following narrative, written by psychoanalyst and author Judith Viorst, provides an example of a luncheon date preempted by a suicide.

> Several years ago a friend and I arranged a lunch date with a distinguished elderly man who had just moved to town, a man who seemed quite unhappy with his new home and the new conditions of his life. My friend and I didn't know him well and I had met him only once, but in asking him out we were not simply being kind. For the man was Bruno Bettelheim, the brilliant and controversial child psychologist, and we anticipated an interesting afternoon. It never happened.
> The morning of our date, when we put in a call to arrange a time to pick him up, we were informed that he was unavailable. We called again and received the same reply. Later that day we learned that Dr. Bettelheim would be permanently unavailable. He had killed himself. (Malikow, 2009, p. 58).

Myth: Many suicides are not planned but occur on a whim.
Counter: While Gernsbacher's assertion that suicide is the culmination of a lifelong process might not be accurate, it would be simplistic to characterize any suicide as a spontaneous act. Redfield-Jamison, author of *Night Falls Fast* (1999), perhaps the most comprehensive book ever written on suicide, believes suicide is a complicated act that is deliberate as well as impulsive. Accordingly, she has written: "Although many suicidal patients have well-formulated plans for suicide, the ultimate timing and final decision to act are often determined by impulse (1999, p. 189). She is not alone in her observation that more often than not, suicide is a premeditated act contemplated over a long period of time and culminated when a "final straw" is added and/or the opportunity presents itself.

Myth: You can tell if people are suicidal by their appearance.

Counter: While it is true that indifference to personal hygiene is an indicator of depression, this is not always the case. The poem "Richard Corey," written by Edward Arlington Robinson, is a literary example of a man whose meticulous appearance belied his suicidal determination:

> Whenever Richard Cory went down town,
> We people on the pavement looked at him;
> He was a gentleman from sole to crown,
> Clean favored, and imperially slim.
>
> And he was always quietly arrayed,
> And he was always human when he talked;
> But still he fluttered pulses when he said,
> "Good-morning," and he glittered when he walked.
>
> And he was rich - yes, richer than a king,
> And admirably schooled in every grace;
> In fine, we thought that he was everything
> To make us wish that we were in his place.
>
> So on we worked, and waited for the light,
> And went without the meat, and cursed the bread;
> And Richard Cory, one calm summer night,
> Went home and put a bullet through his head (2016).

In real life, on January 22, 1987 Pennsylvania State Treasurer Robert Dwyer called a press conference, ostensibly to resign. He was facing up to 55 years in prison and a $300,000 fine for malfeasance. There was nothing in his appearance that hinted of suicide, but after reading a statement reiterating his innocence, he pulled a .357 Magnum revolver from a large envelope and shot himself in the mouth.

Myth: Only insane people commit suicide.
Counter: This statement is another overgeneralization. While many suicides are driven by insanity it does not explain all suicides. Percy Bridgeman, a Nobel laureate and Harvard physics professor,

committed suicide in 1961 when an irreversible illness had sapped his strength. Shortly before his suicide, a colleague reported Bridgeman telling him:

> I would like to take advantage of the situation in which I find myself to establish a general principle; namely, that when the ultimate end is as inevitable as it now appears to be, the individual has a right to ask his doctor to end it for him (Nuland, 1993, p. 153).

Because Bridgeman's physician could not legally euthanize him, Bridgeman shot himself, leaving behind a suicide note that included, "It is not decent for society to make a man do this to himself. Probably, this is the last day I will be able to do it myself" (p. 152). Given his circumstances, Bridgeman's pre-suicidal thoughts are hardly the rants of an insane man. The same can be said of the circumstances of the aforementioned Lawrence Kohlberg. As well, the celebrated longshoreman-philosopher Eric Hoffer showed calm deliberation before attempting his suicide, as described in his memoir, *Truth Imagined* (1983).

Myth: Most people who commit suicide leave a note.
Counter: Perhaps a reason for this myth is the speculation that many suicide notes are withheld or destroyed by family members, many of whom fear a confirmed suicide would preclude a life insurance payment. However, from numerous studies, starting with Shneidman's research in 1944 and continuing to the present, an estimated 25 percent of suicides are accompanied by a note.

Myth: Suicide is not contagious.
Counter: So-called "cluster suicides" are a reality. The December 2015 issue of *The Atlantic* featured a story on a cluster of suicides in California's Silicon Valley where the combined 10-year suicide rate of two of its high schools was four to five times higher than the national rate (Rosin, pp. 63-73). "The tendency for suicide to incite imitation, especially if the death is highly publicized or romanticized, is persistent" (Redfield-Jamison, 1999, p. 278). For this reason, in 1994 the Centers for Diseases Control and Prevention issued

recommendations to the media for reporting suicides. These recommendations included not presenting simplistic explanations for the suicide and not glorifying the suicide or the person who committed it.

Myth: If a person is determined to commit suicide, there is no preventing it.

Counter: In fact, many people who attempt suicide, if restrained, do not attempt again. Richard Selden's study of 515 people restrained from jumping from the Golden Gate Bridge showed that 95 percent of them either were still alive at the time of his study or had died of natural causes (1978). Given the lethality of jumping from this bridge it cannot be argued that the prospective jumpers were engaged in a mere suicidal gesture. Although they intended to die, they did not return to the bridge or go elsewhere to kill themselves.

Myth: A suicide attempt is a cry for help - nothing more.

Counter: This is one of the most dangerous myths if it is believed by someone who is in contact with a suicidal person. A history of suicide attempts is the most accurate predictor of accomplished suicides Chang, 2011, pp. 1-23). Approximately one-fifth of accomplished suicides had a previous attempt and about one-third of people who attempt suicide will try again within one year (Tintinalli, 2010, pp. 1940-1946). Approximately one-tenth of people who threaten or try to commit suicide eventually kill themselves (New York Times, 2017).

"The Bridge," a documentary about suicides and attempted suicides at the Golden Gate Bridge, includes an interview with Kevin Hines, a teenager who survived jumping from the bridge (2007). His survival was improbable; since 1937 only 28 people have survived this jump and an estimated 1,600 have not. Kevin Hines was not merely crying out for help, he expected to die.

However, even a cry for help should be taken seriously. Not just because it is born of desperation, but because it might go awry the next time it is tried. The first page of David Lester's *Making Sense of Suicide* provides this case study:

IV.   Suicide Myths: What Are Some Common Misconceptions About
Suicide?

A married woman of 25, Susan G., is annoyed with her
husband's behavior and decides to teach him a lesson. He
arrives home every evening punctually at 5 p.m. At 4:30 p.m.
she takes a large number of sleeping pills and lies down in the
hallway near the front door of their house. The husband is
injured in a traffic accident on his way home and he does not
come home until late that night. Susan G. dies (1997, p. 1).

Myth: Suicide is not restricted to human beings. There are animals
and insects that also commit suicide.
Counter: This myth is addressed earlier in this book where it is
pointed out the self-destructive behaviors of some animals and insects
do not involve deliberation and hence are not suicidal.

Myth: Children under the age of 12 do not commit suicide.
Counter: The statistics say otherwise. According to the Centers for
Disease Control and Prevention, children in the age range 5 - 14
commit suicide.   Although the rate of suicide is low compared to
other age groups, the frequency of suicide for this group peaked in
1995 and has remained constant since 2004.

Myth: There is a gene for suicide.
Counter: This myth has some fact association. Although a suicide
gene has not been isolated, there is a genetic component to
depression, which can lead to suicide, especially if combined with
previous suicides in a family. The Briggs family is a stunning instance
of this lethal combination:

A man named Edgar J, Briggs, who hanged himself on his
farm, near Danbury, Connecticut, a few days ago, was almost
the last surviving member of a family which has been
practically wiped out of existence by suicide. The history of
self-destruction in this family extends over a period of more
than fifty years, and in that time, so it is stated, at least twenty-
one of the descendants and collaterals of the original Briggs
suicide have taken their own lives. Among these were the
great-grandfather, grandfather, father, brother, and two sisters
of the one just dead (*Medical Record*, 1901, pp. 660-661).

Myth: Antidepressant medications cause suicidal behavior.

Counter: A fundamental principle of logic is: "A" preceding "B" is insufficient to establish "A" as the cause of "B." Consider "A" as taking an antidepressant medication and "B" as suicidality. First, obviously, only a depressed person would be taking an antidepressant. (Why would anyone else take this type of medication?) And, with few exceptions, suicidal people are depressed. Second, it is impossible to know with certainty if everyone who has attempted or committed suicide while on an antidepressant would not have done so if they had not been on this medication. Third, there is virtually no disputing that antidepressants usually have a palliative effect on depression.

In 2004 the Food and Drug Administration issued a public health advisory that antidepressants can cause suicidality in some people, especially adolescents. This so-called "black box warning" is the FDA's strongest measure short of removal from circulation. In addition, there have been over 200 lawsuits against Eli Lilly, manufacturer of the antidepressant Prozac, dating back to 1988 when the drug was introduced. Given the FDA caution and numerous lawsuits, why has Prozac and similar antidepressants remained available? The answer: "The overwhelming majority of evidence indicates that those medicines, though imperfect, have prevented and reduced enormous amounts of human suffering" (Joiner, 2010, p. 245). Moreover, follow-up studies have shown that adolescent suicides have increased since 2004 while antidepressant prescriptions for adolescents have decreased. Studies in other countries have yielded the same result. If these medications are the culprits as some claim then a reduction in their prescriptions should have resulted in a reduction in adolescent suicides.

Since these medications provide the desired effect much more often than not but adversely effect a small subset of patients, what is to be done? Joiner's answer: "What should always have been done and what the FDA advisory urges: people starting on an antidepressant medication should be closely monitored to make sure that the usual therapeutic response and not the unusual overactivation response results" (p. 250).

Myth: The peak season for suicide is Christmas.

IV. Suicide Myths: What Are Some Common Misconceptions About Suicide?

Counter: Intuitively, the winter season in general and Christmas in particular create an environment for an increase in attempted and accomplished suicides. It makes sense that harsh weather, minimal sunlight, and amplified loneliness for those who are alone during the holiday season compose a lethal combination. But in fact in the United States suicides peak in late spring and early summer. One explanation for this is the unsupportable belief of many depressed people that they will feel better when the weather becomes more pleasant. When their mood does not elevate while those around them are invigorated by the balmy weather, the depressed become even more depressed. Since suicides increase in the northern hemisphere in May and June and increase in the southern hemisphere in November sunlight might also be a factor. A possible explanation for this is the hormonal effect of sunlight.

Myth: Life insurance policies include nonpayment of benefits if the death is a suicide.

Counter: This statement is not necessarily true. Although some policies stipulate nonpayment if the cause of death is suicide, others will pay benefits if the suicide occurred two or three years after the purchase of the policy. Another factor is *non-disclosure* of a mental health and/or addiction condition. If at the time of the purchase of the policy the carrier was not informed of these conditions then payment can be denied. Even if an insurance carrier does not ask about these conditions, denial of payment is a possibility. (An insurance company cannot suspend a policy or deny benefits if these conditions are diagnosed after the policy has been purchased.) The death of actor Heath Ledger led to denial of benefits to his daughter even though his cause of death was "acute intoxication." The insurer claimed his death was suspicious, noting the policy had been in effect for only seven months. After a lengthy lawsuit, payment was made.

V.   Suicide Prevention: How Can Suicides Be Anticipated?

No man ever threw away a life while it was worth keeping.
- David Hume

Since the morality of suicide is addressed in chapter XI (Suicide as an Ethical Issue), a defense of suicide prevention is not presented in this chapter. Nevertheless, it should be noted there is disagreement among suicidologists as to whether all suicides should be prevented. Shneidman believed even severely ill patients should be discouraged from committing suicide because wherever there is life, there is hope. In his last book on suicide, authored 23 years after his first, he wrote, "Our constant goal is prevention - but first must come understanding" (1996, p. 7). Lester disagrees, having written:

> We should realize that the quality of life can sometimes be more important than its quantity. There are times when people should not be subjected to prolonged agony followed by inevitable death simply on the grounds that no matter what, "life is sacred" (1997, p. 185).

Implicit in the balance of this chapter are the assumptions that all suicides should be prevented and many suicides are preventable.

Suicidal people can be identified from circumstances and clues. The circumstances are situations or conditions of their life. Clues are behaviors that suggest they are preparing to kill themselves. This is not to say that everyone in these circumstances or who engages in these behaviors is suicidal. What follows are the conditions and actions frequently observed among suicidal people.

Circumstances

There are many types of losses. The death of a loved one can instigate suicidal thinking. If the death occurred suddenly, it can create such despair that a person in mourning might view death as a means for reuniting with the deceased. Death is not the only way in which a relationship comes to an end. A romantic or marital breakup also can be devastating. This kind of loss is well characterized by the adage, "You don't die from a broken heart, but you wish that you could." Loss of bodily functioning owing to blindness, amputation or spinal cord injury can lead to suicidality. In addition, many burn victims live in unremitting physical pain and facial disfigurement to which they cannot acclimate. Unemployment is not merely the loss of a job; it can lead to other losses, including self-esteem and identity.

People can lose control of their life as a result of bad decision-making. A case in point is Brent Wallace, whose story appeared in an Upstate New York newspaper in 1998.

> Brent Wallace took along a .410 gauge shotgun when he drove his Suzuki Samurai to high school Wednesday morning. He found his girlfriend inside Sherburne-Earlville High School and kissed her goodbye, said Cheryl Wallace, Bret's mother.
>
> Brett Wallace ran out of school and drove about a quarter of a mile from the school driveway. He pulled over on Collins Hill Road, took his shirt off and put the shotgun to his head (*The Syracuse Post Standard*, 10/23/1998).

Two days earlier, Brett pled guilty to grand larceny and was sentenced to one to three years in prison.

Imprisonment, a troubled relationship with his girlfriend, and the end of his high school football career drove him to the conclusion that the only way to regain control of his life would be to end it. Incarceration not only means the loss of freedom and control over one's life, it can also be a source of humiliation accompanied by guilt for having disappointed and embarrassed family and friends.

Yet another loss, is the loss of a dream. Although people are often encouraged to never give up on a dream, Judith Viorst offers this wise assessment:

> For the road to human development is paved with renunciations. Throughout our life we grow by giving up. We

give up some of our deepest attachments to others. We must give up certain cherished parts of ourselves. We must confront, in the dreams we dream, all that we never will have and never will be. Passionate investment leaves us vulnerable to loss. And sometimes, no matter how clever we are, we must lose (1986, p. 16).

"Another condition that contributes to suicide is substance abuse. Heavy and increasing use of drugs and alcohol can make it easier for a person to develop a plan for suicide and act on it" (Grollman and Malikow, 1999, p. 62). A person doesn't have to be an addict to be influenced by substances that can cloud judgment and facilitate reckless behavior. Many suicides have been impulsive acts carried out in a drunken or drugged state.

Personal History

Closely related to circumstances is an individual's life story. Previous suicide attempts, physical abuse as a child, a family history that includes an accomplished suicide or mental health history that includes depression imply the possibility of a suicide attempt. Another contributor to suicidality is perfectionism. Self-imposed expectations that are impossible to achieve make disappointment certain, depression probable, and suicide possible. In her memoir singer Judy Collins, who lost her son to suicide, describes her own suicide attempt as a teenager and attributed it to her perfectionism (2003).

Clues

"In addition to circumstances, suicidal people often provide clues that they are moving in the direction of self-destruction. Indications that someone is in a process that will end in suicide include the following" (Grollman and Malikow, 1999, p. 62):

Asking questions about what happens to a person who dies or showing interest in whether there's an afterlife.

V.   Suicide Prevention: How Can Suicides Be Anticipated?

Being preoccupied with music, movies, poems, and books about death.

Showing unusual curiosity about the suicide of a celebrity, friend or classmate.

Declaring the meaninglessness of life and futility of trying to enjoy life in a cruel and unjust world.

Talking about meeting with a physician or member of the clergy without being clear as to why. (Such a meeting might be helpful if the doctor or cleric is familiar with suicidal thinking and competent to provide counseling.)

Contacting people with whom there's been little or no contact for a long time. (This could indicate a desire to directly or indirectly say goodbye.)

Giving away things of personal value that might serve as remembrances.

Isolating from friends and family.

Being disinterested in activities that used to provide pleasure.

Showing indifference to family, work, school, and financial obligations.

Behaving recklessly when driving and/or seeking the company of people who engage in high-risk behaviors.

Showing extremes in eating. (Eating voraciously or experiencing loss of appetite.)

Showing extremes in sleeping. (Sleeping almost continually or being sleep deprived.)

Acquiring the means to commit suicide. (e.g. Acquiring prescription medication without taking it. This is referred to as "stockpiling.")

Insisting on staying behind when the family is going on vacation.

Appearing to feel better after a lengthy period of depression and suicidal talk. (Often, when a person has struggled with whether to live there is relief when the decision to die has been made. This relief is accompanied by a visible elevation of mood.)

Assessing Suicidality

Determining someone's degree of suicidality cannot be done with precision. However, with few exceptions, a suicide attempt is preceded by preparation and there is a progression toward most suicide attempts. The following means of assessment is used by mental health professionals. Of course, honesty on the part of the person being evaluated is helpful but not necessary. A perceptive professional can discern suicidality from the way in which questions are answered and discussed. In addition, this progression can be helpful to concerned friends and family who might be aware of one or more of these four behaviors.

1. Musing: Expressing thoughts of suicide in a general, abstract way. (e.g. "I sometimes wonder if life is worth the struggle," or "Maybe everyone would be better off if I weren't here.")

2. Knowledge of the Means: Knowing how the suicide would be attempted. Unfortunately, some locations provide the means, like the Golden Gate Bridge in California, Niagara Falls, and Cornell University's Fall Creek Gorge.

3. Acquisition or Availability of the Means: (e.g. Purchasing a gun or toxic substance or accumulating potentially lethal prescription medication.)

4. Determination of Time and Place: Knowing specifically when and where the attempt will be made.

What if you've promised not to tell anyone?

Imagine being approached by someone who asks, "If I tell you something will you promise not to tell anyone?" Is it reasonable to expect someone to enter into an agreement without first knowing the terms of that agreement? Lawyers insist no one should sign a contract without fully understanding the contract's requirements. The adage, "Never sign a blank check" is good advice.

A prudent response to this question is, "I can keep a secret if it doesn't involve someone being hurt or killed. Obviously, you have something important to tell me, so why not just tell me?" A refusal to tell should be taken as an intimation of suicide and addressed accordingly. (The next chapter, Crisis Intervention, provides suggestions for how to proceed.) It would be irresponsible as well as dangerous to promise not to tell and keep that promise. In a book about suicide written for teenagers the authors offer the following:

> Life is complicated. We try to manage life by living according to rules. Keeping our word and not breaking promises is one of those rules. Acting to preserve life is another rule. Sometimes rules come into conflict and we are challenged to choose one over the other. If you've already promised not to tell anyone she's suicidal, we urge you to break that promise. It is better to lose a friendship than a friend. You can repair a broken friendship; you cannot apologize to a friend who is dead (Grollman and Malikow, 1999, p. 65).

What if you don't know what to say?

Is there anything helpful that comes from merely listening to a suicidal person? The answer to this question is "yes." Freud and his mentor, Joseph Breuer, referred to their patients' recounting of painful experiences as the "talking cure." For their patients, the emotional release that came from someone listening proved to be therapeutic. The "talking cure" is also referred to as *catharsis*, derived from the Greek word for "purification" or "cleansing."

In the previously mentioned book written for teenagers, the authors explain why listening helps:

> You can never go wrong being yourself. You're not a psychiatrist or a trained suicide crisis counselor. You're a friend of someone who is in such pain and confusion that he wants to die. For reasons that we will never fully understand it always helps to talk. Perhaps it is not what is said but the experience of not being alone that eases the pain and diminishes the confusion.
>
> By being with your friend as a friend you are proving to her that she is not alone. By telling her this, perhaps through your tears, you are demonstrating that she is valuable and loved. By promising to continue to spend time with her as a friend, not a counselor, while she's getting the additional help she needs, you are committing to all that you are able to do for her. You can never go wrong being yourself, and a friend is who you are (1999, p. 66).

VI.   Crisis Intervention: How Can a Suicide Attempt in Progress Be Stopped?

At the sound of the gunshot leave a message.

- Mary Karr

Shneidman has written,

> Every single instance of suicide is an action by the dictator or emperor of your mind. But in every case of suicide, the personality is getting bad advice from a part of the mind, the inner chamber of councilors, who are temporarily in a panicked state and in no position to serve the person's long-range interests (1996, p. 165).

This panicked state constitutes a crisis - a decisive time. In the Mandarin Chinese language the two characters that combine for the English word "crisis" are "danger" and "opportunity." An optimistic view of a suicidal crisis is to see it as an opportunity as well as a danger. "Karen," a case study in Richard Heckler's *Waking Up Alive*, described surviving her suicide attempt as awakening from a trance in which she believed death was her only option:

> I wouldn't recommend suicide. There are so many other ways to wake up. I think it's good just to know you can leave if you want to - a back door, if the pain in life gets so incredible. I risk more and I can tolerate more because I know I'm not trapped. I know that I have an option to get out of that, but suicide is by no means the only choice (1994, p. 198).

Augusten Burroughs, a witty and brilliant writer, contemplated suicide and came to the same conclusion:

> It wasn't that I wanted to kill myself. What I really wanted was to end my life. ... Ending my life didn't mean that I had to die.

... If I ended my life I could start another one. Where things did not happen to me, but I made them happen. Just because people never even think to step outside their life didn't mean I couldn't do exactly that. ... What did I really and truly need to be reborn? Maybe just two things. A door. And then a highway (2012, pp. 99-100).

Another writer of a similar style, Walker Percy, went so far as to propose suicide as a cure for depression. He made a distinction between a "non-suicide" (those who never consider suicide) and an "ex-suicide" (those who have given suicide serious consideration). Concerning the latter, he wrote, "Since he has the option of being dead, he has nothing to lose by being alive" (1983, p. 81). For Percy, an awareness of life's possibilities follows a serious contemplation of suicide:

You can elect suicide, but you decide not to. ...Why not live, instead of dying? You are free to do so. You are like a prisoner released from the cell of his life. You notice that the door to the cell is ajar and that the sun is shining outside. Why not take a walk down the street? Where you might have been dead, you are alive (1983, p. 80).

The suicide attempt of the philosopher Eric Hoffer came to an end when it serendipitously occurred to him that he could have a different life:

Here was an alternative I had not thought of to the deadening routine of a workingman's life in the city. I must get out on the road that winds itself from town to town. Each town would be strange and new; each town would proclaim itself the best and bid me take my chance. I would take them all and never repent.

I did not commit suicide, but on that Sunday a workingman died and a tramp was born (1983, p. 25).

Burroughs offers this advice to those in a suicidal crisis: "If you hate life you haven't seen enough of it. If you hate your life, it's because your life is too small and doesn't fit you. ... However big you think your life is, it's nothing compared to what's out there" (2012, p. 101).

Heckler's "Karen," Burroughs, Percy, and Hoffer agree that an unfeigned contemplation of suicide can result in a willingness to try a different life. Even Shneidman, who categorically disagrees with suicide, believes its contemplation might be beneficial. In the last paragraph of *The Suicidal Mind* he offers a paradox: "Never kill yourself while you are suicidal" (1996, p. 166). Adding,

> You can if you must, think about suicide as much as your mind wishes and let the thought of suicide - the possibility that you could do it -carry you through the dark night. Night after night. Day after day, until the thought of self-destruction runs its course, and a fresh view of your own frustrated needs comes into clearer focus in your mind and you can, at last, pursue the realistic aspects, however dire, of your natural life (p. 166).

While Shneidman was adamantly opposed to suicide, his voice is not the only one to be heard. In stark contrast is that of Thomas Szasz who believed, "Suicide is a fundamental human right" (1973, p. 67.) Lest there be any ambiguity concerning his position, here are a few of his other statements:

> " ... society does not have the moral right to interfere, by force, with a person's decision to commit this act" (p. 67).

> "He who does not accept and respect those who want to reject life does not truly accept and respect life itself" (p. 67).

> "To prohibit what one cannot enforce is to degrade both authority and obedience, thus undermining not only respect for law, but respect for decency. To prohibit suicide is thus the ultimate folly, and the ultimate indecency" (p. 67).

The fundamental question for anyone engaged in a crisis intervention is, "What do you believe about a person's right to commit suicide?" Szasz believed an individual's life is the possession of that individual and the person who commits suicide has the right to do so. But Szasz's argument assumes all suicides have no effect on others. However, this is rarely the case. With very few exceptions, a suicide has an impact on a number of people left behind. A conservative estimate is each suicide creates three "survivor-victims" (Malikow, 1991, p. iii). This means every year 120,000 people experience the loss of someone to self-determined death, aggregating to approximately one million every decade. (Shneidman, quoted in the next chapter, estimated the figure to be two million every decade.) If anyone who commits suicide has a connection, if not an obligation, to someone else then Szasz's assertion is simplistic. English clergyman and poet John Donne was closer to the truth when he wrote:

No man is an island,
Entire of itself,
Every man is a piece of the continent,
A part of the main.
Any man's death diminishes me,
Because I am involved in mankind,
And therefore never send to know for whom the bell tolls;
It tolls for thee (1624).

Anyone who agrees with Donne will be inclined to abort a suicide attempt in progress and those who agree with Szasz will feel no compulsion to intervene. For those who believe intervention is the appropriate action the balance of this chapter provides suggestions.

Heckler has asked, "What drives someone in these final moments, to carry out his or her plan rather than interrupt it? What is the nature of the momentum that continues one forward, often despite considerable obstacles?" (1994, p. 107). The answer is one of four possibilities or some combination of them. (Each is illustrated by a scene from a well-known movie.)

One, the determination to escape what seems to be an otherwise inescapable situation. In "The Shawshank Redemption" the warden of the prison, Samuel Norton, commits suicide when he is about to be arrested for his nefarious deeds. Facing the dilemma of incarceration or death he opted for latter.

Two, the decision to take control of an otherwise uncontrollable situation. In "The Deer Hunter" Robert DeNiro's character, Michael, asks for three bullets when forced into playing Russian roulette by his North Vietnamese captors. Since his death and that of his comrades seemed inevitable, he chose how he would die. (This is a powerful scene that is believed to have provoked real-life suicides.)

Three, the resolution to communicate by action that which is otherwise incommunicable. In an episode of a television series, "The Bold Ones: The Lawyers," a young woman commits suicide on the eve of her wedding. She left behind a suicide note consisting of one word: "Checkmate."

Four, the desperation to kill pain that is otherwise beyond relief. In "Manchester by the Sea" a father who is guilt-ridden owing to the deaths of his three children caused by his carelessness attempts suicide.

In the face of any of these powerful motivations for self-determined death, there are five principles for disrupting a suicide in progress. Each is presented as a verb since crisis intervention requires action. (In the following recommendations the suicidal person is referred to as "the suicide.")

Negotiate

Negotiating in crisis intervention means bargaining with the suicide. Negotiate for something that is specific and will come across as reasonable and feasible. Asking the suicide to "go on living" is too general and will seem daunting. Asking the suicide to live another 10 or 15 minutes to talk with a psychologist, family member or clergyperson is something that will seem doable. Ask if there's anyone with whom they want to speak.

Even in accomplished suicides there was ambivalence. Asking people to live a few minutes longer will connect with the part of them that doesn't want to die. Take care not to make promises that cannot be kept. Such promises are easily recognizable. (e.g. Don't promise, "You won't have to go to the hospital," or "Things will get better very soon.")

Defuse

VI. Crisis Intervention: How Can a Suicide Attempt in Progress Be Stopped?

The longer a suicide is delayed, the less likely it will occur. In an intervention, with each passing minute the suicide moves away from death and toward life. When in doubt as to what to say next, paraphrase what the suicide has just said or think of a question to ask. Be encouraged that in an intervention, time passing is an asset.

Do not try to extend time by saying, "I know how you feel." Autobiography is rarely effective in an intervention. No matter how empathic you might be, one person cannot completely enter into the feelings of another.

Remain

Do not underestimate the value of presence; being present means the suicide is not alone. A word of caution concerning remaining: do not remain if doing so would place you in jeopardy. In the movie, "Scent of a Woman," a young man remains with the suicide even after the suicide threatens to shoot him. (Even though the suicide did not occur, the intervener took an ill-advised risk.) In another movie, "Courage Under Fire," the intervener does the right thing by getting out of the suicide's car before he drives into an oncoming train.

Absorb

Do not meet anger with anger or insult with insult. Simply stated, in an intervention it is not about you. Be prepared to hear criticisms like, "You can't solve my problems," and "You don't really care about me." To the former you might say, "Neither will suicide;" to the latter you might simply respond, "I'm here."

Reframe

Although not a technical term, "framing" in psychotherapy refers to how patients describe their circumstances to themselves. "Reframing" refers to alternative explanations that offer encouragement and nurture optimism, usually offered by the therapist. People in despair tend to recycle their fatalistic thinking. This is one of the reasons why it is dangerous for a suicide to go into isolation.

Reframing requires another person since encouraging, optimistic descriptions are not going to be generated by the suicide.

Since perception is reality, reframing requires sensitivity to the perspective of the suicide. Dismissing or belittling the suicide's framing will be counterproductive and might even end the conversation. "The missing tile syndrome," an analogy created by theologian Dennis Prager, provides an excellent explanation of framing and reframing. When he was in a beautifully tiled bathroom his eyes were drawn to its only apparent flaw. Of the hundreds of tiles decorating the walls there was one missing tile. After he realized his attention had been given disproportionately to the missing tile, he resumed admiring the craftsmanship that produced the room. The missing tile was still there but less obvious to Prager.

Several years ago I received a patient who had been referred following a motorcycle accident. An engineer in his early forties and married with two teenage children, he was suicidal owing to the reality of the remainder of his life as a paraplegic. In the first session he asked, "What is the frequency of suicide among paraplegics?" I responded that it is high relative to the general population in the first year following the spinal cord injury, but no higher after approximately one year. Of course, he asked, "What's going to happen in one year?" I told him after one year he would become accustomed to the inconveniences of life in a wheelchair. Also, he would see his life not in terms of what he lost, but in terms of what he retained and reacquired through occupational therapy. He agreed to give himself one year before committing suicide. A year later we agreed that he no longer needed therapy and it ended with him saying, "I can't believe a year ago I planned on killing myself. I've lost a lot, but I've kept a lot too." He had reframed his life.

Psychiatrist Gordon Livingston defines psychotherapy as, "goal-directed conversation in the service of change" (2004, p. 70). He employs reframing when working with suicidal patients:

> When confronted with a suicidal person I seldom try to talk them out of it. Instead I ask them to examine what it is that has so far dissuaded them from killing themselves. Usually this involved finding out what the connections are that tether that person to life in the face of nearly unbearable

psychic pain. ... Suicide is the ultimate expression of preoccupation with self. Instead of just expressing the sympathy and fear that suicidal people evoke in those around them, therapists included, I think it is reasonable to confront them with the selfishness and anger implied in any act of self-destruction.

Does this approach work to prevent someone from killing himself? Sometimes. In thirty-three years of practicing psychiatry I have lost this argument only once (p. 72).

Livingston redirects his patients' attention to the reason or reasons they have for living since that is what has sustained them to the present. He also redirects their attention away from themselves toward those who will be affected, if not devastated, by their suicide.

VII.   Suicide Postvention: How Can Those Who Have Lost Someone to Suicide Be Helped?

I believe that the person who commits suicide puts his psychological skeleton in the survivor's emotional closet.

- Edwin Shneidman

The term "suicide survivor" lends itself to misunderstanding because it implies someone who has attempted suicide without accomplishing it. Instead, a suicide survivor is someone who is in bereavement over the loss of a relative, friend or associate to suicide:

> Suicide is described as an impersonal act, yet it kills a part of everyone who is close to or loves the person who dies. The emotional pain for the suicide victim is over, but it is only beginning for the survivors (Smith, 1986, p. 5).

The provision of care and comfort for those who have lost someone to suicide is referred to as "postvention counseling." The number of survivors is considerable:

> If there are 50,000 committed suicides in the United States each year - not counting the couple million "subintentioned" presently labeled natural, and homicidal deaths - then there are at least 200,000 survivor- victims created each year whose lives are forever benighted by the event. A comprehensive understanding of the "suicidal problem" obviously has to include postvention along with prevention and intervention in a full-mounted tripartite approach (Shneidman, 1972, pp. x-xi).

Gordon Livingston, the psychiatrist quoted in the previous chapter, is a suicide survivor. His son, at age twenty-two, committed suicide after a lengthy struggle with bipolar disorder. In his grief, which continues to the present, Dr. Livingston has written:

> I imagine that his final desperate moments were eased with some anticipation of release from the anguish he had endured. I pray that he found at last the peace he had sought. Only this hope has allowed me to bear my own pain and go on. ... He chose the too-soon moment of leaving, but I know he loved us as we loved him, and I have forgiven him my broken heart, believing that he forgave me all mistakes as his father (2004, p. 74).

The balance of this chapter addresses four characteristics frequently encountered among suicide survivors:

guilt
needing to know why
anger
fear

Survivors and Guilt

Survivors often believe they should have known or at least sensed that suicide was imminent. This belief might be baseless, but it might also be well-grounded. As is always the case when trying to be helpful, careful listening is essential. The last encounter the survivor had with the suicide might have included hints of self-destruction, but these hints might not have been detectable to an untrained person.

If the survivor's last encounter with the suicide was unpleasant this is unfortunate, but it is highly unlikely to have been the cause or even a contributor to the suicide. The death was a choice made by the deceased and the act of a troubled person who probably did not take advantage of available help. (The suicide of a child is an exception to this description since a child lacks sufficient life experience for responsible decision-making and would not know how to acquire help.)

Survivors and the Need to Know Why

66

A caring person's need to know why the suicide occurred is understandable. The place to start addressing this need is to confirm the coroner determined the death was a suicide. This determination is not always easily made. Shneidman and his colleague, Norman Farberow, developed a procedure for assisting coroners in such cases - a *psychological autopsy*. It is an investigation of the immediate pre-suicide activities of the deceased as well as relevant life circumstances. Interviews with people who knew the suicide and/or were in recent contact with the deceased, a suicide note (if one was left), and the methodology used to end life are part of the investigation. (In 1962 Shneidman and Farberow conducted a psychological autopsy on Marilyn Monroe and declared her death a "probable suicide.")

If a psychological autopsy was performed the results can be requested by the immediate family. If one was not conducted or is unavailable, much of the same information could be acquired informally, albeit unprofessionally. Nevertheless, the discussion and effort might prove helpful to the survivors. A necessary caveat is there is a limit to knowing the inner-workings of another human being, especially one who suffered in silence. Shakespeare's Hamlet spoke for many when he said, "I have that within which passeth show" (Act 1, scene 2).

Survivors and Anger

It is difficult to admit to anger toward someone who committed suicide. To be angry with someone who chose to die might seem insensitive and a survivor might store anger at the unconscious level and be in denial concerning it. This is not to say a survivor should be challenged to admit to it. Instead, it should be proposed as a normal and understandable reaction to being abandoned. This is especially the case when a husband and father or wife and mother leaves the surviving spouse to provide and care for the family alone.

Another possibility is anger toward someone the survivor believes is responsible for the death. Although circumstances created by other people might have been contributing factors, ultimately suicide is a decision made by the deceased. Nevertheless, the survivor's explanation for anger is therapeutic and it merits attention.

VII. Suicide Postvention: How Can Those Who Have Lost Someone to Suicide Be Helped?

Survivors and Fear

When a suicide takes family members by surprise it can give rise to the fear that another will follow.

Genetically linked people, especially if their family history includes other suicides, often wonder if one among them is a suicide in waiting. Suicide recurring in a well-known family like the Hemingways nurture this fear. (The renown poet Sylvia Plath committed suicide in 1963 and her son did the same 46 years later.)

Another source of fear are behaviors that are common among those in mourning. These behaviors can cause people to question their sanity. The constellation of symptoms associated with depression (forgetfulness, sleep disruption, eating disorders, disinterestedness, etc.) can be disturbing as well as disruptive. Sudden bursts of crying or "calling out" the name of the deceased are not unusual. Normal behavior is relevant to circumstances and mourning the loss of someone to suicide is hardly a normal condition.

Practical Help for Survivors

Although this chapter addresses the questions and problems survivors are likely to express, careful listening is essential for being an effective helper. Sometimes the most helpful action is to suggest someone else who is better prepared to be helpful. That person might not be a mental health professional. A doctoral dissertation written in 1991 consisted of research to evaluate the competency of clergypeople for suicide postvention counseling. The researcher was surprised to find they were well-prepared for this work (Malikow, 1991, pp. 76-95).

Other sources of practical help are support groups and reading material. Concerning the latter, the body of material for suicide survivors is impressive. Below is an annotated bibliography of a dozen such books.

An Unquiet Mind, Kay Redfield-Jamison

A renown psychologist, professor, and author, Redfield-Jamison has adapted to life with bipolar disorder. Her struggle with the illness includes an attempted suicide.

Darkness Visible, William Styron
A bestselling author, Styron brought his talent as a writer to the task of describing what it is like to live with a depression that, at times, descends to contemplating suicide.

Lament for a Son, Nicholas Wolterstorff
Wolterstorff, a philosophy professor, lost his son in a mountain-climbing accident. Although his son's death was not the result of a suicide, the value of this book is its articulation of the grief felt at the loss of a child. It articulates the heartbreak many feel but cannot express.

Living When a Young Friend Commits Suicide, Earl Grollman and Max Malikow
Written specifically for teenagers who have lost a friend or relative to suicide, it addresses the issues and questions that are likely in the wake of a suicide.

Making Sense of Suffering, Peter Kreeft
Written from a theological - philosophical perspective, Kreeft responds to the question, "If a loving, benevolent God exists then why is there evil and suffering?" Although an academic (Professor of Philosophy, Boston College), this is a practical book, written with clarity and compassion.

Making Sense of Suicide, David Lester
An eminent suicidologist, Dr. Lester responds to the questions most often asked about suicide. This is a thoroughly researched, well-written treatise on the subject.

Man's Search for Meaning, Viktor Frankl
A classic written by a psychiatrist and Holocaust survivor, the author accomplished his goal with this book. Frankl wrote to

encourage readers that even in the worst of circumstances, an individual can construct a meaningful life.

Night Falls Fast: Understanding Suicide, Kay Redfield-Jamison
Redfield-Jamison's remarkable talent as a writer is on display in this book. Moreover, her thoroughness as a researcher makes this the consummate work on the subject. A serious study of suicide is impossible without reading *Night Falls Fast*.

Sanity and Grace: A Journey of Suicide, Survival, and Strength, Judy Collins
The memoir of the famed singer and songwriter, it is the story how she responded to her son's suicide. She credits Edwin Shneidman for the help he provided as her therapist.

Stronger than Death, Sue Chance, M.D.
This is an especially moving account since the author is a psychiatrist who lost her son to suicide. This book meets the criteria of practicality, clarity, and honesty.

Suicide Myths, Thomas Joiner
Professor Joiner addresses the seemingly numerous myths that surround suicide. As an academic, his presentation is the result of considerable research. As a writer on a mission, he decisively dispels a myriad of erroneous ideas in circulation about suicide.

The Suicidal Mind, Edwin Shneidman
Perhaps no one is better prepared to provide insight into the mind of a suicidal person. This is Dr. Shneidman's last contribution to the field of suicidology, written after a half-century of research, teaching, and clinical work.

When Bad Things Happen to Good People, Harold Kushner
Although not a book about suicide, this is a classic in the field of applied theology and pastoral counseling. It has sold an estimated four million copies since its publication in 1981.

VIII.   Depression and Suicide: What is the Relationship Between Depression and Suicide?

In a sense, and as in melodrama, killing yourself amounts to confessing. It is confessing that life is too much for you or that you do not understand it.

- Albert Camus

The novelist William Styron expressed disdain for the word "depression," feeling it was inadequate to convey the intensity of emotional pain he experienced. He preferred the earlier psychiatric term, "melancholia," and accordingly wrote:

> When I was first laid low by the disease, I felt a need among other things, to register a strong protest against the word "depression." ..."Melancholia" would still appear to be a far more evocative word for the blacker forms of the disorder, but it was usurped by a noun with a bland tonality and lacking any magisterial presence, used indifferently to describe an economic decline or a rut in the ground, a true wimp of a word for such a major illness (1992, p. 35).

Nevertheless, up to the present, depression remains as a part of technical psychiatric vocabulary. Diagnostic criteria for a *major depressive syndrome* have remained constant through revisions of the American Psychiatric Association's *Diagnostic and Statistical Manual*. This diagnosis requires at least five of the symptoms listed below persisting every day for a minimum of two weeks. (At least one of the first two symptoms must be present and the symptoms cannot be attributed to bereavement, substance abuse or a medical condition.)

depressed mood
diminished interest or pleasure in all or most daily activities

significant unintentional weight loss or appetite increase or
decrease
insomnia or hypersomnia
psychomotor agitation or retardation
fatigue or energy loss
feelings of worthlessness or inappropriate guilt
concentration difficulty or indecisiveness
recurrent thoughts of death or suicidality

Sylvia Plath, referred to in the previous chapter, committed
suicide at age 30. In her semi-autobiographical novel, *The Bell Jar*,
she described herself as suffering with a major depressive disorder:

> I hadn't washed my hair for three weeks. ... It seemed silly to
> wash one day when I would only have to wash again the next.
> It made me tired just to think of it. I wanted to do everything
> once and for all and be through with it (1971, pp. 142-143).

This chapter explores the relationship between clinical depression
and suicide by considering explanations for depression, suicide
among creative artists, and suicide among the elderly.

A. Depression and Suicide

It would be simplistic to explain suicide solely in terms of
depression. As stated earlier, while virtually all accomplished suicides
include depression as part of the clinical picture, not everyone with a
major depressive disorder commits suicide. To simplistically attribute
suicides to depression, would be akin to explaining all drownings as
the result of contact with water. Granted, virtually all drownings
include contact with water but not all contact with water results in a
drowning.

The occurrence of a major depressive disorder is 34,000 per
100,000 in the general population in the United States (Kessler et al,
1994). The occurrence of suicide is approximately 13 per 100,000 or
2,615 times less frequent than a major depressive episode. Obviously,
if all people with this diagnosis committed suicide there would be an

astonishingly greater number of suicides than the current 40,000 annually.

The difference between a depressed person who commits suicide and a depressed person who does not attempt suicide is despair. The distinguished psychiatrist Rollo May characterized depression as "the inability to construct or foresee a future" (1969, p. 243). But this is not an accurate depiction of depression since depressed people are able to envision a future. What May characterized as depression is actually a description of despair. Quoted in chapter III is an excerpt from a letter written by Abraham Lincoln in which he describes his depression:

> I am the most miserable man living. If what I feel were distributed to the whole human family, there would not be one cheerful face on earth. Whether I shall ever be better, I cannot tell: I awfully forebode I shall not. To remain as I am is impossible; I must die or be better, it appears to me (Shenk, 2005, p. 56).

Although depressed and, at times, suicidal, Lincoln constructed and envisioned a future. Lincoln's greatness does not reside in overcoming depression and then going on to do great work. Instead he triumphed over his depression by not allowing it to prevent him from doing his duty. Also quoted in chapter III is Joshua Shenk's observation that Lincoln believed "he had been charged with so vast and sacred a trust that he felt he had no moral right to shrink from his responsibilities" (2005, p. 66).

Equally troubled was Henri Nouwen, a Catholic priest and prolific writer. His memoir includes a description of a his seven-month bout with agonizing depression:

> That was a time of extreme anguish, during which I wondered whether I would be able to hold onto my life. Everything came crashing down - my self-esteem, my energy to live and work, my sense of being loved, my hope for healing, my trust in God ... everything. ...
> What had happened? I had come face to face with my own nothingness. It was as if all that had given my life meaning

was pulled away and I could see nothing in front of me but a
bottomless abyss. ...

To my surprise, I never lost the ability to write. In fact,
writing became a part of my struggle for survival (1999, pp.
xiii, xvi).

Like Lincoln, Nouwen did not commit suicide. Also, like Lincoln,
he retained a measure of hope that his work had meaning in spite of
how he felt. Lincoln and Nouwen do not conform to May's depiction
of depression because they were able to construct and foresee a
future. Had they been unable to do so they would have been in despair
and possibly committed suicide. John Maltsberger, past President of
the American Association of Suicidology, believes people are driven
to suicide by despair, not depression (1987). Camus believed the same
and wrote, "A man devoid of hope and conscious of being so has
ceased to belong to the future" (1991, p. 32).

To be depressed is not to be in despair. In depression there
remains at least a smidgeon of hope that something better is in the
offing. In despair there is no balm in Gilead; to be in despair is to be
bereft of hope. Camus said, "We live on the future" (1955, p. 10). In a
state of despair, there is no desirable future.

B. Explanations for Suicide

Two general categories of depression are *endogenous* and
exogenous. Endogenous depressions originate from within, meaning
their origin is biologic. Depressions resulting from an insufficiency of
a neurotransmitter (a chemical messenger that affects mood) are
endogenous. Also endogenous are depressions that are genetic.
Research has established that depression runs in some families. Thirty
percent of children with one parent who has a mood disorder will also
have a mood disorder. Fifty to seventy-five percent of children with
two parents who have a mood disorder will also have a mood disorder
(Halgin and Whitbourne, 2000, p. 285). Twin studies have provided
further evidence that some mood disorders are biologically driven. In
research the term *concordance* means, "if one, then the other."
Regarding mood disorders, fraternal twins have a concordance rate of

approximately 20 percent; identical twins have a concordance rate that is three times higher (p. 285).

Exogenous depressions are attributable to circumstances. A man who has lost his job or a woman experiencing an unwanted divorce are examples of situations that are adequate to explain a depression. Aaron T. Beck, founder of Cognitive Behavioral Therapy (CBT), believes a depression is exogenous if it caused by negative thoughts that are illogical and unsupportable. He refers to these thoughts as "automatic thoughts" that persist until they are challenged. Beck coined the term "cognitive triad" to refer his patients' three categories of negative views: themselves, the world, and the future. He is not positing that all pessimism is unwarranted. It is the misperceptions that are addressed in CBT.

Beck's University of Pennsylvania colleague Martin Seligman has contributed another category of exogenous depression. Seligman attributes some depressions to a "learned helplessness" developed from experience and/or teaching. This type of depression is sustained by the belief that unwanted circumstances cannot be changed or avoided in spite of any effort to do so. A.A. Milne's children's story character, Eeyore, is a fictional example of depression owing to learned helplessness. Eeyore is the gloomy, anhedonic donkey recurringly moaning, "What the use?" Seligman believes this type of depression lends itself to Cognitive Behavioral Therapy because if helplessness can be learned, it also can be unlearned.

Freud's structure of the human psyche as consisting of the *id, ego,* and *superego* is well known and foundational to psychoanalytic theory. According to Freud the superego is the "parent" in all of us that guides our behavior in matters pertaining to right and wrong. Speaking imprecisely, it is the conscience, although they are not identical. If the superego is overdeveloped it means the sense of right and wrong is amplified, rigid, and excessively demanding. An overdeveloped superego can generate guilt and depression for thoughts and behaviors that are not morally wrong.Closely related to the overdeveloped superego is *perfectionism*. Perfectionism is not the pursuit of excellence, rather it is a commitment to doing everything perfectly in order to live above criticism. Perfectionists are especially vulnerable to depression because their "standards are high beyond reach or reason" (Antony and Swinson, 2009, p. 10). Alasdair Clayre,

author, musician, and perfectionist, committed suicide the day before
the publication of a book he had worked on for several years.

> Professor Clayre ended his life by jumping into the path of
> a train at the Underground station in North London. According
> to his friends he had been mortally fearful of what reviewers
> might say about his book.
> Professor Clayre's death was largely due to a relentless
> perfectionism, in the judgement of Dr. Sidney J. Blatt, a
> psychologist at Yale University. Dr. Blatt cites the suicide ...
> as testimony to the dark side of unrelenting standards for
> achievement. ... (Perfectionists) are implacable self-critics,
> vulnerable to overreacting to what they perceive as failure,
> often to the point of depression (Goleman, 1996).

Existential angst is yet another source of depression. (*Angst* is the
German word for anxiety or dread.) It is the awareness of the
possibility that life has no meaning, causing an extreme form of
anxiety leading to a feeling of despair and hopelessness. This
awareness also leads to the realization that each individual is
responsible for constructing a meaningful life. Unfortunately, this
realization creates anxiety as well. Carl Jung recognized this in his
patients and wrote,

> Among my patients from many countries, all of them educated
> persons, there is a considerable number who came to see me,
> not because they were suffering from a neurosis, but because
> they could find no meaning in life or were torturing
> themselves with questions which neither present-day
> philosophy nor religion could answer (1934, p. 231).

C. Suicide Among Creative Artists

A study of geniuses (I.Q. 140 or higher) conducted by Shneidman
in 1969 produced an astounding result. Of the 1,528 children
identified as geniuses in 1921, 28 of them had committed suicide by
1969. The occurrence of suicide among this group was 65 times
greater than that of the general population. Expressed differently, if

the general population's occurrence rate was that of this genius group, it would be 1,832 suicides per 100,000 rather than the actual 12 per 100,000.

Granted, the geniuses in Shneidman's study were not a standard random sample representing all geniuses. Also stipulated is a high I.Q. is not synonymous with creative genius, although it correlates with some expressions of genius. (Howard Gardner's *Theory of Multiple Intelligences* posits there are nine types of intelligence.) Nevertheless, it is reasonable to assume intelligence and extraordinary creative accomplishment correlate. Redfield-Jamison has investigated this relationship and found that "highly creative individuals are much more likely than the general population to suffer from depression and manic-depressive illness" (1999, p. 180). In addition, she has written, "Suicide is more common in highly creative or successful writers, artists, scientists, and businessmen than it is in the general population. Most are related to underlying depression, or alcoholism in combination with these mood disorders" (pp. 180-181).

Ernest Hemingway's suicide three weeks before his 62nd birthday is an example of a confluence of these factors. In 1961 he took his life as did his father, brother, and sister. The suicide of his granddaughter brought the total of Hemingway suicides to five over four generations. His suicide was preceded by years of substance abuse (alcohol) and an unrestrained lifestyle. In addition, he had manic-depressive illness, the same illness that plagued his father, Clarence, and son, Gregory. Eventually Hemingway spiraled downward to a state of despair when he could no longer write. Invited to participate in President Kennedy's inauguration, the man who had produced some of the greatest novels in literary history was unable to write even a few sentences for the occasion. His suicide must have seemed imminent when he said to a friend, "writing is the only thing that makes me feel that I'm not wasting my time" (Hotchner, 1966, p. 144).

In the introduction to *Touched with Fire: Manic-depressive Illness and the Artistic Temperament,* Redfield-Jamison wrote:

> The main purpose of this book is to make a literary, biographical, and scientific argument for a compelling association, not to say actual overlap, between two temperaments - the artistic and the manic-depressive - and ...

the importance of moods in igniting thought, changing
perceptions, creating chaos, forcing order upon that chaos, and
enabling transformation (1993, p. 8).

Ten years before his own suicide David Foster Wallace wrote an
essay entitled, "The Depressed Person." Its first paragraph describes
the ineffable pain of depression:

The depressed person was in terrible and unceasing emotional
pain, and the impossibility of sharing or articulating this pain
was itself a component of the pain and a contributing factor in
its essential horror (1998, pp. 57-64).

In a commencement address given seven years later, Wallace
made a brief allusion to suicide:

It is not the least bit coincidental that adults who commit
suicide with firearms nearly always shoot themselves in ... the
head. And the truth is that most of these suicides are actually
dead long before they pull the trigger (2005, pp. 58-59).

The poet William Cowper made the same observation
following one of his several suicide attempts:

Encompass'd with a thousand dangers,
Weary, faint, trembling with a thousand terrors ...
I ... in a fleshly tomb, am
Buried above ground (2017).

D. Suicide Among the Elderly

The statistics are striking: In 2014 the suicide rate for people 85
years-old or older was 19.3 per 100,000 (The 2014 suicide rate for the
general population was 13.4 per 100,000.) This was not an anomaly;
in the last sixty years the suicide rate of this group of elderly has been
consistently 50 percent higher than the general population. In
addition, the statistics are virtually the same for those between the

ages 75 and 84 with one year, 1950, showing a suicide rate of 31.1 per 100,000 compared to 13.2 for the general population.

What factors account for the high rate of suicide among the elderly relative to other age groups? A starting point for answering this question is to apply Maltsberger's previously cited explanation for suicide: "Not anger, but rage; not depression, but despair; not loneliness, but aloneness" (1987). A literary example of elderly rage is Mary Carson, a character in Coleen McCullogh's *The Thornbirds*. Mary is a once beautiful woman embittered in her old age. Hopelessly in love with Father de Bricassart, a Catholic Priest half her age, she rails against God when declaring her love to de Bricassart:

> "I have loved you," she said pathetically.
>
> "No you haven't. I'm the goad of your old age, that's all. When you look at me I remind you of what you cannot do, because of age."
>
> "You're wrong, I have loved you. God how much! Do you think my years automatically preclude it? Well, Father de Bricassart, let me tell you something. Inside this stupid body I'm still young - I still feel, I still want, I still dream, I still kick up my heels and chafe at restrictions like my body. Old age is the bitterest vengeance our vengful God inflicts on us. Why doesn't he age our minds as well?" She leaned back in her chair and closed her eyes, her teeth showing sourly. "I shall go to Hell, of course. But before I do, I hope I get the chance to tell God what a mean, spiteful, pitiful apology of a God He is!" (1979, p. 182).

Gernsbacher's *The Suicide Syndrome* describes the aloneness and despair of Rose Ashby:

> Rose Ashby walks to the dry cleaners to pick up her old but finest dinner dress. Although shaken at the cost of having it cleaned, Rose tells the sympathetic girl behind the counter, "Don't worry. It doesn't matter. I won't be needing the money anymore." ...

VIII. Depression and Suicide: What is the Relationship Between
Depression and Suicide?

Back in her apartment Rose washes and sets her hair. It's good she has to do it herself. Look at this hair. So thin, so sparse, so frowsy. What would a hairdresser think?

Then makeup. Base. Rouge. Lipstick. Bright red. Perfume? No! No cheap perfume for Rose today. Remember the bottles of *Joy* Chet would buy for her? He always wanted her to have the best. ...

Where is the *Joy* now? Dead and gone. With Chet. Rose manages a wry laugh at the play on words.

Slipping into her dinner dress she looks into the dresser mirror. "It's good you can't see this face now, Chet. How old and ugly it looks."

Taking some lavender notepaper from the drawer, she stands at the dresser to write. Why didn't anyone warn her that growing old was like this? It is so unfair. But they don't care. People don't care about anyone except themselves. ...

Trying to relax, Rose arranges the folds in her skirt as she settles down on the chaise. Carefully sipping the water as she takes all the capsules so as not to smear her lipstick, Rose quietly begins to sob. After a lifetime of tears, these will be her last. Her note on the dresser is short, written to no one and everyone.

You don't know what it is like to have to grow old and die (1988, p. 227-228).

Rose Ashby and Mary Carson have "ceased to belong to the future;" both women are "devoid of hope and conscious of being so" (Camus, 1991, p. 32). In a word, they are in despair. Despair for the elderly is encapsulated in the oft quoted closing lines of a T.S. Eliot poem:

I grow old ... I grow old ...
I shall wear the bottoms of my trousers rolled.

Shall I part my hair behind?   Do I dare to eat a peach?
I shall wear white flannel trousers, and walk upon the beach.
I have heard the mermaids singing, each to each.

I do not think that they will sing to me (2017).

Approximately one in five suicide attempts by the elderly results in death. Although firearms are the most common methodology, the elderly are less likely to survive a suicide attempt owing to frailty. "A young person might survive an overdose that proves lethal to an older adult," according to James Ellison, a geriatric psychiatrist (Levingston, 2014). In addition, the elderly can effect suicide by indifference to life-prolonging treatment and medication. They fit Shneidman's description of *death-welcomers*, who desire to end life by not taking medication or engaging in other life-sustaining treatments.

Another expression of indifference is disinterestedness in pleasurable activities. The Hebrew Bible describes King David as stopping for death in his last days:

> When King David was very old, he could not keep warm even when they put covers over him. So his attendants said to him, "Let us look for a young virgin to serve the king and take care of him. She can lie beside him so that our lord the king may keep warm."
> Then they searched throughout Israel for a beautiful young woman and found Abishag, a Shunammite, and brought her to the king. The woman was very beautiful; she took care of the king and waited on him, but the king had no sexual relations with her (1 Kings 1:1-4, NIV).

Anyone familiar with the life of King David is aware of his proclivity for sexual engagement with beautiful women. His disinterestedness in Abishag as anything other than a human blanket signaled his death was imminent.

IX.   Adolescent Suicide: Why Are Teenagers Especially Vulnerable to Suicide?

There is no despair so absolute as that which comes with the first moments of our first great sorrow, when we have not yet known what it is to have suffered and be healed, to have despaired and have recovered hope.

- George Eliot

Although the suicide rate for young people ages 15 to 19 is lower than the general population, the frequency is still arresting. In 2010 the occurrence was 7.5 per 100,000. Approximately 18 percent of all deaths in this age group are suicides, the third leading cause behind accidents and homicides. Seven-hundred adolescents attempt suicide each day with 14 resulting in death.

What accounts for those who have lived less than one-fourth of their life expectancy committing suicide? A feasible explanation is the tendency of adolescents to engage in some or all of four types of thinking that contribute to despair and suicide ideation. These tendencies produce exaggerated assessments and histrionic displays. (This is not to say there are no adults who do this, certainly there are and those who do are susceptible to the same downward spiral.)

Global vs. Specific Thinking: Global thinking is characterized by gratuitous statements like, "Everybody hates me," and "I can't do anything right." It is overreactive and given to overgeneralizations.

Permanent vs. Temporary Thinking: Assessing a temporary problem as permanent discourages addressing the problem. "What's the use?" is the rationale for not trying to confront the issue.

Immediate and Total vs. Process and Partial Thinking: Even if some problems cannot be solved completely, they can be solved partially. And even if some problems cannot be solved immediately, they can be solved eventually. Life experience, which adolescents lack, teaches many of life's setbacks call for damage control. A related life lesson is not every dream will come true, but some dreams can be altered and realized in a different form.

External vs. Internal Locus of Control: People who abdicate control over a situation over which they actually have some influence are nurturing *learned helplessness*, a dependable path to depression. Those who vainly hope that other people or luck will make things better perpetuate the problem and reinforce their self-perception as impotent and incompetent.

Serious But Not Suicidal

Three behaviors observed among adolescents that provide insight into their suicidality are self-mutilation ("cutting"), anorexia nervosa, and autoerotic asphyxia ("the choking game"). Although none of these behaviors are unique to adolescents, they are overrepresented in this age group. While these behaviors are not suicidal per se, understanding their motivations is helpful in understanding adolescent suicide.

It is always wrong to characterize a behavior as nonsense because every behavior is intended to satisfy a need. Viewed in this way every behavior makes sense. Self-mutilation is an attempt to meet at least one of three needs: reconnection, distraction or relief. The self-infliction of pain ends the eerie experience of being dissociated from one's own body. The pain reconnects "cutters" with their body, ending the numbness. A second motivation is the need to be distracted from a terrifying feeling. The "cutter" who feels anger escalating to rage or sadness moving toward despair feels the need to stop the process. The intuition that rage could lead to murder or despair to suicide compels an action that will abort the progression. A third motivation is the need to experience relief from overwhelming anxiety. Human beings are unique in the ability to attach meaning to rituals. Just as Christian believers experience a feeling of forgiveness from the sacrament of Holy Communion, "cutters" experience a feeling of relief when watching blood flow from a self-inflicted wound.

Ironically, each of these behaviors prevents suicide. If any of the needs that drive them were to continue unabated a suicide attempt might occur. This does not mean self-mutilation should be encouraged. Rather, it should be replaced with an alternative means of relief that is not maladaptive.

Another maladaptive behavior with informative implications for suicide is *anorexia nervosa,* an eating disorder characterized by an intense fear of gaining weight, obsession with extremely low bodyweight, and a distorted perception of the body (dysmorphia). People with anorexia make an extraordinary effort to control their weight by severely reducing food intake and, in many cases, vomiting after eating. Other weight control measures are extreme exercise and overusing laxatives and diuretics.

Although anorexia is categorized as an eating disorder, it isn't about food. Instead, it is an unhealthy means for coping with emotional problems. Often, the need for control drives the illness. In many cases females who have been sexually abused hate their body and anorexia is a way of regaining control by not yielding to their body's need for food. In other cases, anorexia is an expression of rebellion against over-controlling parents. In such cases the implicit statement is, "Eating is the one thing you cannot force me to do." A trenchant piece written by Augusten Burrough's shows an understanding of the relationship between control and anorexia. In it he speculates what he would do if he had an anorectic daughter for whom all treatments had proven ineffective:

> I would kick her out of the house.
>
> I would give her a credit card and an ATM card attached to a bank account that held the money I had saved for her college, along with anything else I had planned on giving her.
>
> I would tell her I loved her. Then I would tell her I was finished raising her. That she would have to take over from now on.
>
> I would explain that I was no longer going to be a part of her treatment. I was no longer going to be a part of her life. She could be a part of mine, if she wanted and if she made all the effort. But she was free to make no effort at all; I had accepted the loss. I no longer wanted anything from her or for her.

IX.   Adolescent Suicide: Why Are Teenagers Especially Vulnerable to Suicide?

I would say these things even if saying them brought me four inches from death by heartbreak.

But an exaggerated, magnified - even savagely abrupt - removal of anything that could even remotely be distorted into "guidance" might be the very thing needed to save her (2012, p. 54).

Autoerotic asphyxia is a third type of serious, non-suicidal behavior engaged in by adolescents. As with self-mutilation and anorexia nervosa, autoerotic asphyxia is found among other age groups. Notwithstanding, between 1995 and 2007 at least 82 children and adolescents died in autoerotic asphyxiation accidents (U.S. Centers for Disease Control and Prevention). Most of these deaths occurred within the age group 11 to 16. Colloquially referred to as "the choking game," it requires a scarf or belt around the neck and gradual lowering of the body (usually from a doorknob) while masturbating. The decrease in oxygen and increase of carbon dioxide in the brain intensifies the orgasm. Unintentional death results from passing out before completion of the act. Suicidal asphyxia is distinguished from autoerotic asphyxia accidents when the victim is nude, cross-dressed or found with genitals exposed or accessible.

Precise statistics as to the occurrence of such deaths are unavailable owing to the reluctance of next-of-kin to disclose the cause-of-death. An example from drama is the movie "World's Greatest Dad" in which a father, portrayed by Robin Williams, discovers his son's body following an autoerotic asphyxia accident. Not wanting to humiliate his son posthumously, the father carries out an ill-fated cover up (2009). The exotic is erotic and the willingness of children and adolescents to explore that which is sexually intriguing makes them especially vulnerable to autoerotic accidents. Another factor is the incomplete development of the brain's frontal cortex, making this age group more disposed to experimenting without carefully weighing possible consequences.

The Agony of Inferiority

In *Preparing for Adolescence* psychologist James Dobson wrote:

But what is this problem which so many adolescents face at this time of life? ... It's a feeling of hopelessness we call 'inferiority.' ... What a shame that most teenagers decide they are without much human worth when they're between thirteen and fifteen years of age! (1978, p. 16).

What accounts for this feeling of inferiority? Dobson maintains parents, teachers, peers, and the media unwittingly conspire to communicate to children there are three characteristics that give value to a person: beauty, intelligence, and talent. Borrowing from the Olympic Games, he refers to these as the *three coins of human worth* with beauty being the gold, intelligence the silver, and talent the bronze. He believes this message is planted in childhood and takes root in adolescence.

Concerning the most prized coin, he points to children's stories in which beauty is integral to a happy ending. (e.g. *Beauty and the Beast, Snow White and the Seven Dwarfs, Cinderella,* and *The Ugly Duckling*) Ellen Berscheid and Elaine Hatfield address the issue of "beauty and the best" in their book, *Interpersonal Attraction* (1969). The unintended consequence of the message that at least one of these gifts is integral to a good life is a feeling of inferiority for many of the children who are not so endowed. Singer-songwriter Janis Ian captured this feeling in her Grammy Award winning song "At Seventeen:"

> I learned the truth at seventeen
> That love was meant for beauty queens
> (Ian, 1974).

Cluster Suicides

Cluster suicides are suicides inspired by a previous suicide. A 1987 study of youth suicide by the Centers for Disease Control found that 1 to 5 percent of all youth suicides occur in clusters. Referred to in chapter IV is the article in *The Atlantic* addressing the ten-year suicide rate of two Silicon Valley high schools that were four and five times higher than the national average (Rosin, 2015).

IX. Adolescent Suicide: Why Are Teenagers Especially Vulnerable to Suicide?

The unanticipated suicide of a friend or peer is a traumatic experience for many teens leaving them bewildered. The suicide of one teen might influence others who have contemplated the meaning of life if not suicide. Media influences, including the suicide of a well-known celebrity or idol can have a similar influence on depressed young people (This is referred to as the *Werther Effect*, derived from a Johann von Goethe novel in which one suicide provoked another). For this reason, Redfield-Jamison cautions the media against romanticizing a suicide or disclosing how it was accomplished (1999, pp. 280-282).

The opening of Charles Dickens' *A Tale of Two Cities* provides an apt characterization of adolescence:

> It was the best of times, it was the worst of times, it was the age of wisdom, it was the age of foolishness, it was the epoch of belief, it was the epoch of incredulity, it was the season of Light, it was the season of Darkness, it was the spring of hope, it was the winter of despair, we had everything before us, we had nothing before us, we were all going direct to heaven, we were all going direct the other way ... (1999, p. 1).

Emotionally, adolescence is a time of extremes and extreme emotions provoke extreme behaviors. Suicide is one such behavior.

When Sue Chance, a psychiatrist, lost her son to suicide she wondered what she had missed as a mother and mental health professional. In *Stronger than Death: When Suicide Touches Your Life*, she wrote about the harm and danger of incorrectly thinking there is no compensation for poor parenting. Reflecting on the parenting she received, she wrote,

> I do not like my parents and I do not like the things they did to me. However, I am responsible for who I am now. There is no way I can reasonably say that, at forty-nine, I am more a product of the first fifteen years I spent with them than I am of the past thirty-four years I have spent with myself. I would, in fact, be very ashamed of myself if it were true (1992, pp. 146-147).

Her advice to adolescents is,

> ... you're getting closer and closer to the time in your life when you can take over and make it better for yourself. That's going to be your choice: whether you stay stuck in blaming and moaning about all the things that have been unfair or get on with it and do the best you can with what you have (p. 146).

Chance agrees with Shakespeare's observation, "How poor are they that have not patience! What wound did ever heal but by degrees?" (*Othello*, Act II, Scene 3). She is disquieted by the impatience of those who commit suicide rather than wait for healing. This is especially true of adolescents, who have so much time to heal.

X.   Altruistic and Rational Suicides: Are the Terms Altruistic Suicide and Rational Suicide Misnomers?

Greater love has no one than this, that he lay down his life for his friends.

- John 15:13

So convenient a thing it is to be a reasonable creature, since it enables one to find or make a reason for everything one has a mind to do.

- Benjamin Franklin

For well or ill, my daughter's early childhood included a father who was writing a doctoral dissertation on suicide. When she was five she asked the inevitable question, "Dad, what is suicide?" I told her that suicide is the word for when someone decides to die and then does something to make it happen.

"Oh," she responded, "you mean like Jesus?"

As noted earlier, one of Durkheim's four categories of suicide is *altruistic.* Self-sacrifice is the defining feature of this type suicide in contrast to an *egoistic suicide* in which there is an extreme sense of self and no sense of obligation to others. An altruistic suicide is a self-determined death motivated by what is perceived as a service to another person or other persons. Chapter II offers an example of an altruistic suicide from Kay Redfield-Jamison's memoir, *An Unquiet Mind*, in which a jet pilot sacrificed his life for the safety of others. The pilot could have saved his life by ejecting from his malfunctioning plane leaving it to crash in a schoolyard where children were playing.

The headline of a 1995 *The Washington Post* story reads: "Mother picks death to continue her life through son's birth." It was the story of a mother who chose to discontinue the aggressive treatment of her cancer that would have aborted her baby:

Clementine Geraci, three months pregnant, made the decision of her life when doctors told her last spring that her breast cancer had spread. She could fight the cancer aggressively and have an abortion, or she could take the less hazardous cancer drugs and carry the baby to term. ... Geraci, known as Tina, died Monday, March 6, at Washington Hospital Center, where she worked as a resident in obstetrics and gynecology. She was 34. ...During most of her pregnancy, Geraci took taxol, which doctors thought would not harm Dylan (her son). She had to stop taking the drug in the seventh month of her pregnancy, and Dylan was born one month prematurely by Caesarean section, during which doctors discovered cancer in her liver. She resumed treatment, but it was too late (*The Washington Post*, March 7, 1995).

In *The Pursuit of Happiness* psychologist David Myers provides this narrative of altruism:

With Nazi submarines sinking ships faster than the Allied forces could replace them, the troop ship *SS Dorchester* steamed out of New York harbor with 904 men headed for Greenland. Among those leaving anxious families behind were four chaplains, Methodist preacher George Fox, Rabbi Alexander Goode, Catholic priest John Washington, and Reformed Church minister Clark Polling. Some 150 miles from their destination, a U-456 caught the *Dorchester* in its cross hairs. Within moments of a torpedo's impact, reports Lawrence Elliot, stunned men were pouring out from their bunks as the ship began listing. With power cut off, the escort vessels, unaware of the unfolding tragedy, pushed on in the darkness. On board, chaos reigned as panicky men came up from the hold without life jackets and leaped into overcrowded lifeboats.

When the four chaplains made it up to the steeply sloping deck, they began guiding men to their boat stations. They opened a storage locker, distributed life jackets, and coaxed men over the side. In the icy, oily smeared water, Private William Bednar heard the chaplains preaching courage and found the strength to swim until he reached a life raft. Still on board, Grady Clark watched in awe as the chaplains handed out the last life jacket, and then, with ultimate selflessness, gave away their own. As Clark slipped into the waters he saw the chaplains standing – their arms linked – praying, in Latin, Hebrew, and English. Other men, now serene, joined them in a huddle as the *Dorchester* slid beneath the sea (Myers, 1992, p. 196).

Some have argued altruism is a concept without a corresponding reality because every act of unselfish regard for others is tainted by self-interest. They argue since Mother Teresa experienced satisfaction from obedience to her calling and joy in her work then her concern for others was mixed with self-gratification. Moreover, if she carried on her ministry without any sense of self-sacrifice then her work lacked a necessary component of altruism. However, such reasoning is specious because altruism is defined as "concern for the welfare of others, as opposed to egoism" (*American Heritage Dictionary*, 1973, p. 39). There is nothing in this definition that requires an altruistic act to be unadulterated. Altruistic is a word in common usage and readily understood to describe the spirit in which an act is performed.

Ayn Rand posited that altruism's actual existence does not establish it as a virtue.

> The Objectivist ethics holds that *human* good does not require human sacrifices and cannot be achieved by the sacrifice of anyone to anyone. ...Altruism holds *death* as its ultimate goal and standard of value – and it is logical that renunciation, resignation, self-denial, and every other form of suffering, including self-destruction, are the virtues it advocates. And, logically, these are the only things the practitioners of altruism have achieved and are achieving now (Rand, 1964, pp. 34, 37-38).

However intellectually appealing Rand's argument might be, the visceral reaction to the unnamed pilot, Clementina Geraci, and the four chaplains is their actions are deserving of commendation. Altruism, not egoism, is the ubiquitous virtue. No culture honors absolute self-preservation but every culture recognizes generosity and concern for others.

What motivates an altruistic suicide?

The obsolete Hindu practice of *suttee* in which a widow expressed devotion to her husband by committing suicide at his funeral or shortly thereafter is an instance of suicide motivated by duty. Americans became familiar with another form of suicide in the line of duty during World War II when Japanese kamikaze pilots intentionally flew their explosive laden planes into targets. (*Kamikaze* derives from the Japanese words for *divine* and *wind*.)

A self-determined death can motivated by love. When Jesus spoke the words, "Greater love has no one than this, that he lay down his life for his friends" (John 15:13) he was anticipating his execution. He also spoke of his imminent death as part of his mission and, therefore, his duty: "Now my heart is troubled, and what shall I say? 'Father, save me from this hour?' No, it was for this very reason that I came to this hour" (John 12:27).

Kohlberg's *moral stages theory* consists of six stages of reasoning ranging from simplistic and concrete to abstract and principled. Stage six reasoning is characterized by an individual's perception of unqualified ethical principles. The United States Marine Corps motto, "Death before dishonor" and its Japanese Samurai warrior counterpart, *seppuku*, are principles by which soldiers place their honor and duty above the preservation of their life. Obedience to these codes of conduct could result in death in the line of duty as well as death on behalf of a comrade.

Words have definitions and usages; the former are found in dictionaries and the latter in lexicons. The three sacrificial deaths referred to earlier meet the criteria for *suicide* (the act or instance of intentionally killing one's self) and *altruistic* (characterized by a concern for the welfare of others as opposed to one's own). History speaks favorably of those who have sacrificed their lives for others. In the Gettysburg Address Abraham Lincoln honored soldiers "who gave their last, full measure of devotion" (2017). During the Battle of Britain, Winston Churchill expressed his nation's debt to the pilots of the Royal Air Force with the words, "Never in the field of human conflict was so much owed by so many to so few" (2017). The Reverend Dr. Martin Luther King, Jr. went so far as to say, "I submit to you that if a man has not discovered something that he will die for, he isn't fit to live" (2017).

If altruistic suicides exist, are they morally right actions?

Ethical philosophy has two general ethical categories: *teleological* and *deontological*. Derived from the Greek word for "end" (*telos*), a teleological approach to ethics evaluates an act in terms of the desired goal. In the case of the Air Force pilot, his goal was to avert a tragedy. By staying with the plane it did not crash in the schoolyard. Therefore, teleologically, his action was morally right. The same can be said of Tina Geraci. Since the goal of the four chaplains was to save lives as well as actualize their faith and encourage men facing death then the chaplains displayed moral uprightness

Derived from the Greek word for duty (*deon*), a deontological approach to ethics measures rectitude in accordance with ethical principles or a code of moral conduct. Deontologically, the pilot, Tina Geraci, and the four chaplains demonstrated virtue, each in accordance with a different principle. The pilot acted as a soldier who was responsible to protect and serve. Tina Geraci displayed a mother's sacrificial love for her child. As clerics, the chaplains conducted themselves as men called to human service, acting in obedience to their understanding of what God required of them.

As a mental health professional I have spent many hours with suicidal patients. Over the years, I have said to many of them, "You will never get my encouragement to kill yourself." However, I have never been with a pilot in a plane bearing down on a schoolyard or counseling a cancer ridden, pregnant woman or consulting with chaplains on a sinking ship. Because of them and others like them I believe *altruistic suicide* is a concept with a corresponding reality.

Can a suicide be rational?

An action is rational if it is based on or agrees with accepted principles of logic. A characteristic of a rational act is that it is determined by reason rather than emotion. Can a suicide be the result of a well-reasoned process untainted by emotion? If the question is framed in this way the answer is *no* because emotion is a factor in every suicide. If the question is simplified to whether a suicide can result from a well-reasoned process then the answer is *yes*.

This being said, it must be added that people sometimes reason correctly from an incorrect premise. Someone who commits suicide because of believing something that is not true might have acted rationally but in error. Sherwin Nuland, a physician, addressed this possibility concerning the elderly who erroneously believe their depression is untreatable:

> I have more than once see a suicidal old person emerge from depression, and rediscovered thereby a vibrant friend. When such men or women return to a less despondent vision of reality, their loneliness seems to them less stark and their pain more bearable because life has become interesting again and they realize that there are people who need them (1995, p. 152).

Rational suicide is not an oxymoron. This is not to say suicide is a morally right act. (Suicide as a moral issue is addressed in the next chapter.) Few people are as clear-thinking as the brilliant social philosopher Eric Hoffer. At midlife he weighed and considered his future and, like Macbeth, could see only a "petty pace from day to day" (*Macbeth*, Act V, Scene 5). It is impossible to read Hoffer's description of his suicide attempt and conclude it was the act of an irrational man:

> As the end of 1931 approached, the time came to decide what I would do when the money was gone. Actually, my mind was already made up: I would commit suicide. All I had to do was settle the details. I had to find the means of a quick, painless death. A revolver was ideal, but it was not be had without a police permit. Gas might leak into adjoining rooms and alarm the neighbors. Death by jumping from a bridge or being run over seemed crude. There remained poison (1983, p. 22).

Hoffer proceeded to investigate which poison would accomplish his suicide rapidly with minimal pain. He settled on oxalic acid and bought a large quantity for twenty-five cents. His intention was to walk to the edge of the city, ingest the acid crystals, and quietly die alone.

> I adjusted the bottle against my arm and thought feverishly, "It would be good if this street had no end - I would walk on forever, and my feet would never tire; neither would I fret nor complain." ... There seemed nothing so pleasant as walking on roads, legs and hands swinging, and the knapsack rocking gently. I did not know then that the vision of life as an endless road was the first intimation of a revulsion against suicide (p. 24).

What followed was Hoffer's serendipitous realization that he did not hate life, but he did not want the life he was living. After spitting out the ingested crystals he envisioned a different life. Recall his epiphany, also quoted in chapter VI:

> Here was an alternative I had not thought of to the deadening routine of a workingman's life in the city. I must get out on the road. Each town would be strange and new ... I would take them all and never repent.
> I did not commit suicide, but on that Sunday a workingman died and a tramp was born (p. 25).

Augusten Burroughs, also referred to in chapter VI, likewise realized he did not have to die to end his life. He left his family, relocated to another part of the country, and changed every other changeable thing in his life, including work, friends, and even his name. Burroughs offers an incisive etiological assessment of some suicides: "Suicide isn't always performed in relief of pain - but in a kind of bleak exhaustion as both something to do and a way to block tomorrow from happening again" (p. 98).

XI.   Suicide as an Ethical Issue: Is Suicide a Morally Wrong Act?

Suicide is not an abomination because God has forbidden it; it is forbidden by God because it is abominable.

- Immanuel Kant

"you've got to live," people say ... But do you have to live? Do you always have to be there just because you were there once?... suicides tear to pieces a prescription of nature and throw it at the feet of the invisible prescriber.

- Jean Amery

Once upon a time there was a man sent by his king to recruit archers for the king's army. The man searched far and wide but could not find even one man sufficiently skilled with a bow-and-arrow to serve the king. Finally, coming upon a small village, the man took delight in what he saw. What he saw were targets painted on the sides of numerous buildings, trees, and hillsides. Especially pleasing to him was that each of the targets had an arrow in the dead center, "bull's eye" location. Excited, he asked the first villager he encountered, "Who is the master archer who lives in this village? He is needed for the king's army."

The man of the village responded, "We have no master archer in this village!"

The king's agent then asked, "But what about all these targets with arrows in the dead center?"

The villager replied with a laugh, "Oh, those! Those are from Shlomo, our village idiot. He goes around shooting arrows all over the place and then paints a target around them wherever they land."

One of the six subcategories of philosophy is ethics - the principles of virtuous conduct. There are two fundamental ethical systems: *teleological* and *deontological*. The former determines moral rectitude according to goals. A teleological approach to ethics is summarized by the well-known maxim: The end justifies the means.

The latter determines moral uprightness according to standards that pre-exist an action. In the parable of the village idiot, Shlomo is acting in a manner that is right from a teleological perspective since the goal is a "bull's eye." However, the irony in the story is Shlomo establishes a standard that conforms to his prior behavior. From a deontological perspective, his methodology is flawed and his conduct is wrong.

Psychology, philosophy, theology, and the law are concerned with human behavior. Psychology investigates why people behave as they do. Philosophy, theology, and the law are concerned with how people ought to behave. Psychologists make claims from research; philosophers acquire their insight from reflection; theologians claim knowledge from revelation; and jurists evaluate behavior according to conformity to statutes. Suicide can be discussed psychologically, philosophically, theologically, or forensically. In this chapter the act of suicide is considered as a philosophical topic.

Suicide Considered Teleologically

In chapter III Maltsberger's tripartite analysis of suicide is presented: "Why do people commit suicide? Not anger, but rage; not depression, but despair; not loneliness, but aloneness" (1987).

Recall Dr. Edward Van Dyk who jumped to his death from the fifteenth floor balcony of a Miami hotel after having thrown his four and eight year-old sons over the railing to their deaths. The explanation offered for this unspeakable tragedy was Dr. Van Dyk's conflict with his wife.

This was rage. Also recall Harvard professor and Nobel Prize recipient Percy Bridgman, 79 years-old and suffering with cancer, who shot himself and left behind a note that included, "It is not decent for Society (sic) to make a man do this to himself. Probably, this will be the last day I will be able to do it myself (Nuland, 1995, p. 152). This was despair. Judas Iscariot, alienated from the master he betrayed, isolated from the brotherhood of the eleven other disciples, scorned by the Pharisees with whom he had colluded, "went away and hanged himself" (Matthew 27:5). This was aloneness.

Shneidman, reflecting on over forty years of research on suicide, wrote:

As I near the end of my career in suicidology, I think I can now say what has been on my mind in as few as five words: Suicide is caused by psychache. Psychache refers to the hurt, anguish, soreness, aching psychological pain in the psyche, the mind (1993, p. 147).

Psychache is the emotional pain for which there is no opiate; it is responsible for the drama in the mind that drives suicidal thinking. Van Dyk, Bridgman, and Judas all suffered with psychache, each for a different reason.

In addition to rage, despair, and aloneness, other expressions of psychache are guilt, humiliation, and meaninglessness. Judith Guest's bestselling novel, *Ordinary People*, is the story of Conrad Jarrett, a suicidal adolescent who is overcome with guilt having survived the boating accident in which his brother drowned. The Hebrew historical book II Samuel recounts the suicide of King Saul, who fell on his sword to avert his torture and humiliation at the hands of the Philistines. Reminiscent of Ecclesiastes' refrain in the Hebrew Bible, Carl Jung diagnosed meaninglessness as the psychiatric-philosophical problem of many of his patients. Suicide to end the painful states of rage, despair, aloneness, guilt, humiliation, or meaninglessness is right - teleologically speaking. However, teleologically is not the only way to address suicide.

Suicide Considered Deontologically

As previously stated, deontology derives from the Greek word for duty. Religious prohibitions of suicide are grounded in one's duty to be obedient to the deity or deities. The biblical injunction, "Thou shalt not kill" includes the killing of one's self (Exodus 20:13; Deuteronomy 5:17). Owing to the sacredness of life, the Hindu teaching *ahimsa* requires nonviolence to all living things. In Islam, suicide is forbidden because it violates kismet - one's appointed destiny. The martyred Lutheran pastor, Dietrich Bonhoeffer, reasoned similarly: "God has reserved to Himself the right to determine the end of life, because He alone knows the goal to which it is His will to lead it" (Grollman, 1988, p. 21).

XI.   Suicide as an Ethical Issue: Is Suicide a Morally Wrong Act?

In his *Summa Theologica* St. Thomas Aquinas gave three reasons why suicide is unlawful: it is contrary to the law of nature; it injures the community; and it is usurpation of a divine prerogative.

The philosophical arguments against suicide offered by Socrates and Plato derive from their conviction that human beings are the property of the gods and, therefore, have no right to do away with that which belongs to the gods. Plato wrote:

> I believe that this much is true: that the gods are our keepers and we men are one of their possessions ... So, if you look at it in this way I suppose it is not unreasonable to say that we must not put an end to ourselves until God sends some compulsion (Plato, 1962, p. 105).

The British jurist Sir William Blackstone considered suicide an act of disobedience against the laws of God and man: " ... the suicide is guilty of a double offence, one spiritual, in invading the prerogative of the Almighty, and rushing into His presence uncalled for; the other temporal, against the king, who hath an interest in the preservation of all his subjects" (1765-69, Book IV).

"Hard cases make bad law" is a maxim among jurists (Holdsworth, 1926, IX, p. 423). To establish a principle that addresses the morality of suicide from hard cases would be unwise. Those who take that approach would find themselves, eventually, firmly of two minds. The hard cases that follow are intended to underscore the complexity of the issue and the impossibility of reaching an unassailable conclusion.

Suicide is morally wrong when it is a permanent solution to a temporary problem. Dr. Shneidman has written:

> Every single instance of suicide is an action by the dictator or emperor of your mind. But in every case of suicide, the person is getting bad advice from a part of the mind, the inner chamber of councilors, who are temporarily in a panicked state and in no position to serve the person's long-range interests (1996, p. 165).

The suicidal person who can reframe a seeming hopeless situation into one that is hopeful can move from despair and meaninglessness to a more optimistic view and expectation of better things to come. Quadriplegic artist Randy Souders was challenged to reframe his life at age seventeen when he injured his spinal cord in a diving accident. "At the early stage (of rehabilitation) ... so many things are closed to you," reflected Souders (Smith and Plimpton, 1993, p. 147). Determined to direct his attention to what he could do rather than what he could not, he is now a painter with over 1,500 galleries that have carried his work. Reframing can take a person from the despair of the life that is to the possibilities of the life that could be. Suicide is morally wrong when one presumes that his or her future is set when it is not.

Also, suicide is morally wrong when responsibilities to survivors are abandoned. It is no small matter when a parent commits suicide, relegating the surviving spouse to single-parent status and introducing children to suicide as a coping mechanism.

The suicide of a mentally ill person is a psychiatric event, not a moral failure. In March of 1995, after closing hours at the National Zoo in Washington, D.C., Margaret Davis King cleared several barriers to the lions' outdoor enclosure. The thirty-six-year-old woman's mutilated body was found the following morning, barely recognizable as a human corpse. Not surprising is that she was a homeless woman with a psychiatric history that included paranoid schizophrenia. To consider her death as an ethical issue would be irrelevant to anything meaningful.

Shneidman has written:

> Suicide occurs when the psychache is deemed by that person to be unbearable. This means that suicide also has to do with different thresholds for enduring psychological pain (1993, p. 147).

A serious consideration of whether suicide is a morally wrong act creates an appreciation for the complexity of the issue. A wry definition of dilemma attributed to Oscar Wilde is a situation in which no matter what you choose, you'll be wrong. Those who are forced to choose between ineffable suffering without hope of relief and self-administered death find themselves in a dilemma as defined by Wilde.

XII.   Thanatology: Is it a Bad Thing to Die?

Sleep is good, death is better, but of course,
The best would be never to have been at all.

- Heinrich Heine, "Morphine"

That we age and leave behind this litter of dead, unrecoverable selves
is both unbearable and the commonest thing in the world - it happens
to everybody.

- John Updike

Several years ago I heard two men arguing. At the apex of their dispute one said to the other, "I'm going to kill you!" The other responded, "The way my life is going, death would be an upgrade." Might death *ever* be an upgrade or is it invariably a bad thing to die? Possibly death is neither good nor bad; perhaps it is neutral.

In the first chapter of *Mortal Questions*, Thomas Nagel asks, "If death is the unequivocal and permanent end of our existence, the question arises whether it is a bad thing to die" (1979, p. 1). Like Professor Nagel, in this chapter death is assumed as nonexistence (*annihilation*), a "mere blank," as he characterized death in his writing. This approach reduces the question to a mere consideration of the end of life itself without speculation about postmortem status.

Based on the premise that something is bad if it destroys something good, it is reasonable to assert that death is bad because it destroys life (life being good). However, not every life is good. The approximate 40,000 annual suicides in the United States is compelling evidence that at least that number of people do not consider their life to be good. No doubt, many of them complained, "I did not ask to be born and now I am in an unchosen situation with innumerable other conditions not of my choosing" (Malikow, 2014, p. 28). The painfulness of life is such that some, like David Benetar, advocate *antinatalism*, "the belief that it is immoral to have children because they are not consulted about their entrance into the world" (p. 29). Antinatalists contend every life includes considerable pain, regardless of the pleasure that is experienced. Hence, we are *Better Never to Have Been* (Benetar, 2006). An antinatalist could argue that death is good because it brings to an end something bad - life.

Epicurus aphoristically expressed his belief that death is nonexistence: "Death does not concern us, because as long as we exist, death is not here. And when death does come, we no longer exist" (2016). If something is bad for us only when we are affected by it and if death is nonexistence then death cannot be bad because after death we have no sensation. While the prospect of death might be disturbing, the arrival of death begins nonexistence. Nagel seems to disagree with this reasoning, positing that even if death is nonexistence its badness resides in bringing to an end "all the good that life contains" (Nagel, 1979, p. 1). For him, even a painful life includes some things that are good, however few they might be. Therefore, death is bad because it deprives the deceased of whatever good he was experiencing. But how can this be? If death is a "mere blank" (the premise of this chapter), there is no one who is being deprived. Deprivation is an experience and there can be no experience without an experiencer. Without a plaintiff there can be no case against death. By analogy, a psychiatrist who has written a book in which the secrets of a deceased patient are disclosed does no harm to the patient. If the patient no longer exists, there is no one being deprived of physician - patient confidentiality. A similar analogy is a deceased person whose last will and testament is not honored. In this case there is no one to experience disappointment and betrayal. (In neither of these analogies is it suggested that others would not be harmed by the doctor's disclosures or the misadministration of the will.) Deprivation will be further addressed later in this chapter.

Neither the Apostle Paul nor Socrates thought of death as a bad thing. In the *New Testament*, The Apostle Paul taunted death when he rhetorically asked, "Where, O death is your victory? Where, O death is your sting?" (1 Corinthians 16:55, NIV). He believed heaven is the destination for those who die as followers of Christ. At Socrates' trial for corrupting the youth of Athens by not believing in the gods he faced death unafraid. As recorded in Plato's *Apology*, Socrates hypothesized death either as an eternity of undisturbed sleep or relocation to a place of better existence:

Let us reflect in another way, and we shall see that there is great reason to hope that death is a good, for one of two things: either death is a state of nothingness and utter unconsciousness, or, as men say, there is a change and migration of the soul from this world to another. Now if you suppose that there is no consciousness, but a sleep like the sleep of him who is undisturbed even by the sight of dreams, death will be an unspeakable gain. For if a person were to select the night in which his sleep was undisturbed even by dreams, and were to compare with this the other days and nights of his life, and then were to tell us how many days and nights he had passed in the course of his life better and more pleasantly than this one, I think that any man, I will not say a private man, but even the great king, will not find many such days or nights, when compared with the others. Now if death is like this, I say that to die is gain; for eternity is then only a single night. But if death is the journey to another place, and there, as men say, all the dead are, what good, O my friends and judges, can be greater than this? If indeed when the pilgrim arrives in the world below, he is delivered from the professors of justice in this world, and finds the true judges who are said to give judgment there, Minos and Rhadamanthus and Aeacus and Triptolemus, and other sons of God who were righteous in their own life, that pilgrimage will be worth making. ...What infinite delight would there be in conversing with them and asking them questions! For in that world they do not put a man to death for this; certainly not. For besides being happier in that world than in this, they will be immortal, if what is said is true (Plato, 399 B.C.E.).

Another contribution to the argument that it is not a bad thing to die is the impossibility of imagining what it is like to be dead. Just as it is impossible to imagine what it is like to be unconscious or in the undisturbed sleep to which Socrates alluded it is impossible to conceptualize the experience of death. If death is nonexistence and, therefore, unawareness, then *not being* is something no one among the living can conceive. By definition, a *being* cannot imagine *not being*.

XII.   Thanatology: Is it a Bad Thing to Die?

An interesting, relevant question concerning *not being* is, "If it is bad for us not to exist after death why is not also bad for us not to exist before birth?" Nagel addressed this asymmetrical question when he wrote: " ... none of us existed before we were born (or conceived), but few regard that as a misfortune" (1979, p. 2). Mark Twain also weighed in on this issue with his inimitable, wry humor:

> Annihilation has no terrors for me, because I have already tried it before I was born - a hundred million years - and I have suffered more in an hour, in this life, than I can remember to have suffered in the whole hundred million years put together. There was a peace, a serenity, an absence of all sense of responsibility, an absence of worry, an absence of care, grief, perplexity; and the presence of a deep content and unbroken satisfaction in that hundred million years of holiday which I look back on with a tender longing and with a grateful desire to resume when the opportunity comes (Neider, 1990, p. 49).

Prenatal nonexistence is not the same as postmortem nonexistence. First, the life I might have had if I had been born earlier would not have been my life. Except for having been born a few minutes or even several weeks earlier, the life I might have had owing to an earlier birth would be so different from my actual life that it would be the life of another person. For instance, had I been born in 1839 instead of 1949 I might have fought and died in the Civil War instead of teaching at Syracuse University and fathering my delightful daughter. There is no inherent loss in a prenatal life that might have been because such a life never existed, rendering no loss to me or anyone else.

Second, something that never existed produces no results. Similarly, someone who never existed experiences no loss (or anything else). Expressed musically, "nothing (a life that never existed) from nothing (events that never happened) leaves nothing (Preston and Fisher, 1974). As Nagel argued,

> (I)f there is a loss, someone must suffer it, and he must have existence and specific spatial and temporal location even if the

108

loss itself does not. The fact that Beethoven had no children may have been a cause of regret to him, or a sad thing for the world, but it cannot be described as a misfortune for the children he never had (1979, p. 4).

Another situation that offers an opportunity to explore the possibility of death as a bad thing is a near fatal accident that left a man in a persistent vegetative state (PVS). As an unresponsive patient on a respirator and feeding tube, he is kept alive only through these interventions. After ten years in this state, the man dies. Assuming he had no mental activity while comatose, what would have been the difference *to him* between immediate death in the accident and the death he actually experienced ten years later? What badness did death add to his comatose existence? If there is a difference *to the man* between immediate death and death preceded by a coma, how is this difference described?

In a sense, no death is untimely. Like the Ghost of Christmas Yet to Come in Charles Dickens' *A Christmas Carol*, death arrives in its own time. Still, some deaths are referred to as untimely when they occur before the anticipated eighty or ninety years of life. Again, the question arises, for whom are these deaths tragic? Certainly it is not for the deceased. Viktor Frankl died at 92; King David had a son who lived only six days. Frankl had a long, productive life that touched millions of people. The name of David's son is not given in the biblical passage that describes his brief life; perhaps he died without a name. The impact of the infant's death on David is writ large in the Hebrew Bible (2 Samuel 11,12; Psalm 51). Dr. Frankl's four page obituary in *The New York Times* is a testimony to the significance of his life and implies a great number of people were saddened by his passing. But neither he nor the infant experienced death as a bad thing for himself. Although Frankl and David's son did not have lives of equal length, both will be dead forever. The unpleasantness is experienced by the bereaved.

A poet has written, "For all sad words of tongue or pen, the saddest are these, 'It might have been'" (Whittier, 1856). According to contemporary philosopher Shelly Kagan, w*hat might have been* is the ground upon which death can be considered a bad thing even for the deceased. In his treatise on death, he cautions, "it actually takes some work to spell out exactly how nonexistence could be bad for me" (2012, p. 210). This work includes answering the question, "What is badness?" Kagan and others subdivide badness into three categories: *intrinsic*, *instrumental*, and *comparative*. Something is *intrinsically bad* if it is bad in and of itself. For example, a migraine headache is intrinsically bad because it is painful. Something is *instrumentally bad* if it produces bad results. Kagan offers unemployment as an example of something bad because of what it might cause:

> Losing your job, for example, is not intrinsically bad - it's not bad in and of itself - but it is instrumentally bad, because it can lead to poverty and debt, which in turn can led to pain, suffering, and other intrinsic bads (p. 211).

Death cannot be intrinsically bad because it is nonexistence. Hence, in death nothing painful or anything else is experienced. Neither can death be instrumentally bad because it leads to nothing; its only consequence is not existing.

But Kagan proposes *comparative badness* applies to death, having an impact even on the deceased. Comparative badness exists when something is bad in comparison to something else that might have been. An example is an athlete who wins a bronze medal (third place) at the Olympic Games. Although a laudable accomplishment, a bronze medal is bad in comparison to the gold medal (first place) to which the athlete aspired, making the bronze medal comparatively bad. According to Kagan, comparative badness does not require awareness by the deceased. He concedes the dead are unaware of all the good that might have been, but posits they are no less deprived. Since death dispossesses them of the longer life they might have had, it is a bad thing for them to have died. Concerning this, Kagan offers an explanation:

> Something can be bad *comparatively*. Something could be bad because of what you're not getting while you get this bad thing. It could be bad by virtue of what economists call "opportunity costs." It's not that its intrinsically bad, or even that its instrumentally bad; it's bad because while you're doing this, you're not getting something better (p. 211).

In the movie, "The Unforgiven," Clint Eastwood's character, William Munny, an aging outlaw and murderer, reflects, "It's a hell of a thing, killing a man, taking away all he's got and all he'll ever have" (1992). This is Kagan's argument, presented in drama. Death is bad for the man killed because it takes from him "all he'll ever have." Compared to life, the dead are deprived of whatever good a longer life would have provided.

But this argument is specious. Jack Kerouac died at 47 of complications from alcoholism, thereby depriving himself and others of the books he might have written. But does this nonexistent Kerouac care about those books? How could he? He doesn't exist. The deprivation belongs to the living who would have enjoyed those books. It is true that life acquaints us with the good we will leave behind when we die. But to leave these things behind does not mean we will miss them when we are gone. We would have to exist in order to miss the good with which life has acquainted us.

Professor Kagan's advocacy of the *deprivation theory* by asserting death is comparatively bad is somewhat intellectually appealing. Nevertheless, his argument is not compelling, even to him, and he admits to having some reservation about his position:

> So when I appeal to the deprivation account, and say that the central thing about death is the fact that you're deprived of the good things in life, I don't mean to suggest that everything is sweetness and light with regard to the deprivation account. I think there are some residual puzzles - questions that have not yet been completely answered - about how it *can* be that death is bad (2012, p. 232).

Kagan seems to assume the conclusion of the argument he is making. He alludes to questions that will have to be answered *before* it can be explained why death is a bad thing for the deceased, yet he has already decided that it is. This constitutes begging the question.

Moreover, this issue calls for the application of the Principle of Ockham's Razor, which teaches explanations should be as uncomplicated as possible. In the present case there is no need to summon *comparative badness* into this fray. The simpler, more defensible analysis rests on the irrefutable premise that the dead do not experience the better that might have been. Nagel has written, "The trouble is that life familiarizes us with the goods of which death deprives us" (1979, p. 5). The dead have no troubles; troubles are the possessions of the living. Nagel's analysis of the deaths of John Keats and Leo Tolstoy also applies to Kerouac's death at age 47.

> The death of Keats at age 24 is generally regarded as tragic; that of Tolstoy at age 82 is not. Although they will both be dead forever, Keats' death deprived him of many years of life which were allowed to Tolstoy; so in a sense Keats' loss was greater (though not in the sense standardly employed in mathematical comparison of infinite quantities). However, this does not prove that Tolstoy's loss was insignificant. Perhaps we record an objection only to evils, which are gratuitously added to the inevitable (p. 5).

To observers, the deaths of these three men at their respective ages are variously unfortunate. But to Keats, Tolstoy, and Kerouac, his own death ceased to be a bad thing the moment it arrived.

XIII.   Suicide Notes: What Can Be Learned From Suicide Notes?

The calm,
Cool face of the river
Asked me for a kiss.

- Langston Hughes, "Suicide Note"

"Research indicates that somewhere between 10 and 35% of suicide victims leave notes" (Evans and Farberow, 1988, p. 213). A statistic commonly offered concerning the frequency of suicide notes is 25 percent. These statistics raise the question of why most suicides do not leave behind written parting thoughts. One explanation is many suicides are impulsive acts. After a lengthy period of contemplation the fatal act is spontaneous owing to a rush of emotion or seductive opportunity. Another explanation is many suicides are provoked by a mental illness, usually a mood disorder. In these suicides the decedents lack the concern, ability or energy to compose a suicide note.

In Shneidman and Farberow's landmark study of suicide notes a select group of people were asked to imagine they were about to commit suicide and write a suicide note (1957, pp. 251-256). Their notes were compared to actual suicide notes provided by the Los Angeles County Coroner.

They discovered that the real notes contained more anger, more hostile feelings, and more desire for revenge than the fake notes. The genuine notes also included more concrete instructions to survivors and used more specific names for people, places, and things. The notes, it seems, served as a means for reaching out to specific individuals, of trying to influence and even control them after the writers' deaths (Evans and Farberow, 1988, p. 213).

Forty years after the study Shneidman reported returning to the coroner's office to read recently written notes "to see whether the contents of suicide notes had changed at all in the 40 years since I first studied them" (1996, p. 14). He learned they had not.

Suicide notes often express a culmination of years of despair. "In this respect suicide notes have been thought by some observers to be windows to the mind of the deceased" (Maris, Berman, and Silverman, 2000, p. 266). Even when this is the case it is not the individual's last communication. It is the accomplished suicide that is the desperate last attempt at communication when all other means have failed.

The length of suicide notes ranges from very brief to astonishing length. Before hanging himself in his church a minister wrote, "God forgive me" (Etkind, 1997, p. 13). Mitchell Heisman, a nihilistic philosophy student, left behind a 1,904 page tome elaborating on the meaninglessness of life (Abel, 2010).

Any attempt to classify suicide notes is doomed to omit categories into which some notes could be placed as well as others that qualify for placement in more than one category. Given these disclaimers, the balance of this chapter consists of examples of ten types of suicide notes.

<u>Altruistic</u>

Alex C. wrote to his wife and then committed suicide after a nine-year dispute with the IRS.

My dearest,
I have taken my life in order to provide capital for you. The IRS and its liens which have been taken against our property illegally by a runaway agency of our government have dried up all sources of credit for us. So I have made the only decision I can. It's purely a business decision. I hope you can understand that. I love you completely ... (Etkind, p. 33).

Note: Alex's wife, Kay, used the insurance money to continue the battle with the IRS. Eventually, the court ruled the IRS was in error and Alex and Kay owed nothing.

Ambivalent

A seventy-year-old man who jumped from the Golden Gate Bridge:

Why do they leave this so easy for suicide? Barbed wires would save a lot of lives (p. 60).

Angry

Sara Teasdale's poem, "I Shall Not Care," was published 18 years before her death. However, because she died from an overdose of sleeping pills this poem is often erroneously considered her suicide note. Although it might not have been directed toward a lover who rejected her in real life, it is exemplary of an angry suicide note.

> When I am dead and over me bright April
> Shakes out her rain drenched hair,
> Tho you should lean above me broken hearted,
> I shall not care.
> For I shall have peace.
> As leafy trees are peaceful
> When rain bends down the bough.
> And I shall be more silent and cold hearted
> Than you are now (1933).

Ann Wickett Humphrey wrote to her husband, Derek Humphrey, founder of the Hemlock Society, a "right-to-die" group that advocates for the liberalization of euthanasia.

Derek:
There. You got what you wanted. Ever since I was diagnosed with having cancer, you have done everything conceivable to precipitate my death ...You will have to live with this until you die. May you never, ever forget. Ann (Etkind, 1997, p. 11).

XIII.   Suicide Notes: What Can Be Learned From Suicide Notes?

Note: Following her suicide Derek took out a half-page ad in *The New York Times* stating his wife had a history of emotional problems and the Hemlock Society has never advocated suicide for reason of depression.

Apathetic

Hunter Thompson, Author

"Football season is over." No More Games. No More Bombs. No More Walking. No More Fun. No More Swimming. 67. That is 17 years past 50. 17 more than I needed or wanted. Boring. I am always bitchy. No Fun for anybody. 67. You are getting Greedy. Act your old age. relax. This won't hurt (Brinkley, 2008).

George Eastman, Inventor:
To my friends, my work is done. Why wait? *GE* (Lindsay, 2013).

George Sanders, Actor:
Dear World, I am leaving because I am bored. I feel I have lived long enough. I am leaving you with your worries in this sweet cesspool. Good luck (2017).

Exhaustion

Jerzy Kosinski, Author and Holocaust Survivor:

I'm going to put myself to sleep now for a bit longer than usual. Call the time Eternity (Breitbart and Rosenfeld, 2011).

Ralph Barton, Artist (excerpts):

Everyone who knows me and who hears of this will have a different hypothesis to offer to explain why I did it. Practically all of these hypotheses will be dramatic - and completely wrong. ... I have run from wife to wife, from house to house, and from country to country, in a ridiculous effort to escape from myself. ... (Kellner, 1991, p. 213)

Fatalistic

Percy Bridgeman, a Harvard professor and Nobel laureate, committed suicide at age 79 when he was in the final stages of cancer. Unable to work, he shot himself and left behind a note that included:

It is not decent for society to make a man do this to himself. Probably, this is the last day I will be able to do it to myself (Nuland, 1995, p. 152).

Freddie Prinze, Comedienne:

I must end it. There's no hope left. I'll be at peace. No one had anything to do with this. My decision totally (Prinze, 2017)

Guilt

Charles Stuart claimed the car in which he and his wife, Carol, were returning home was car-jacked by a black man in Boston's inner city. Mrs. Stuart, who was pregnant, was shot and killed and her husband wounded. As racial tensions in the city escalated, it was discovered that it was Stuart who shot his wife and then himself. Stuart committed suicide the day after his brother told the police that Charles murdered Carol and their unborn baby to collect on a life insurance policy.

To my family and friends, I love you very much. Thank you for standing beside me. My life has been nothing but a battle for the last four months. Whatever this new accusation is, it has beaten me. I've been sapped of my strength.
Chuck (1993).

Note: It is not unusual for guilt suicide notes to omit statements of confession or remorse.

In 1987 Robert "Budd" Dwyer was facing a 55 year sentence for accepting a bribe as Pennsylvania State Treasurer. In a press conference at which he was expected to announce his resignation, he pulled a .357 Magnum revolver from a manila envelope and shot himself in the mouth. Like Charles Stuart, his final statement did not include a confession. The following is excerpted from his 21 page statement:

> I've repeatedly said that I'm not going to resign as State Treasurer. After many hours of thought and meditation I've made a decision that should not be an example to anyone because it is unique to my situation. ...
>
> Please leave immediately if you have a weak stomach or mind since I don't want to cause physical or mental distress. ...
>
> Goodbye to you all on the count of three. ... (Muha, 1988).

Note: Subsequent investigations have resulted in uncertainty that Dwyer actually was guilty of malfeasance.

Instructional

Dave Deurson, professional football player, who was diagnosed with CTE (chronic traumatic encephalopathy), a brain diseased related to playing football:

Please, see that my brain is given to the NFL's brain bank (Schwarz, 2011).

Adolf Hitler (excerpts):

It is my most sincere wish that this bequest be duly executed. ...

I myself and my wife - in order to escape the disgrace of deposition and capitulation - choose death. It is our wish to be burnt immediately on the spot where I have carried out the greatest part of my daily work in the course of twelve years' service to my people.

- Adolf Hitler, Fuhrer, Germany

Given in Berlin, 29th April, 4:00 a.m.
Signed: A. Hitler

Signed as witnesses:
Dr. Joseph Goebbels
Martin Bormann
Colonel Nicholaus von Below
(Hitler, 2017).

Note: Hitler's note also could be classified as fatalistic given its reference to "the disgrace of deposition and capitulation." The eminent psychologist Henry Murray, who had been commissioned by the United States government during World War II to construct a personality assessment of Hitler, predicted Hitler's suicide if German defeat became imminent.

A Fourteen-Year-Old Girl (excerpts):

To whom it may concern,
... I have no money, except $2.95 in the bank ... . This is to be given to Robert C_____, my nephew. My clothing goes to charity or anyone who wants them.
If I am laid out I would like to be dressed in blue. If I have a funeral all my friends and are invited to attend. ...
No one has killed me. I wish to die. I have committed suicide (Redfield-Jamison, 1999, p. 79)

Lucy Maude Montgomery, Author (excerpts):

This copy is unfinished and never will be. It is in a terrible state because I made it when I had begun to suffer my terrible breakdown of 1940. ... If any publishers wish to publish abstracts from it under the terms of my will they must stop here. ... May God forgive me and I hope everyone else will forgive me even if they cannot understand (2008).

Note: There is disagreement concerning her death. Her granddaughter maintains her grandmother committed suicide by a drug overdose after years of severe depression. The last sentence of what some believe to be her suicide note reads, "What an end to a life in which I always tried to do my best." Montgomery's biographer believes the so-called suicide note is actually a journal entry and the cause of death to have been coronary thrombosis.

Love

Albert Marsh, Jr. committed suicide in the parking lot of the funeral home where Sue Ann Riggs' body lay in preparation for her funeral. The day before she was murdered by her husband after he discovered Sue Ann and Marsh were having an affair. This brief note was found with a box of roses on the front seat of Marsh's car:

I am sorry I have to do this. Life without Sue is nothing. These roses are for Sue (Malikow, 2016, p. 13).

Kurt Cobain, Musician:

Frances and Courtney, I'll be at your altar. Please keep going Courtney, for Frances for her life will be so much happier without me. I LOVE YOU. I LOVE YOU. (Cobain, 2017).

Virginia Woolf, Author (excerpts from her letter to her husband, Leonard):

> Dearest, I feel certain that I am going mad again. I feel we can't go through another of those terrible times. And I shan't recover this time. ... You have been in every way all that anyone could be. ... What I want to say is I owe all the happiness of my life to you. ... If anybody could have saved me it would have been you. ... I can't go on spoiling your life any longer. I don't think two people could have been happier than we have been. V (Woolf, 2017).

Philosophical

Jo Roman, an artist and social worker, coined the term rational suicide. She not only advocated euthanasia but also the right to choose the time of one's own death. She committed suicide at age 62 after being diagnosed with a treatable breast tumor. Her philosophy is expressed in the following excerpts from her suicide note:

> ... More than a decade ago I concluded that suicide need not be pathological. Further, that rational suicide makes possible a truly ideal closing of one's life span. Commitment to a rational suicide spares one erosive accelerating investment against unwanted existence.
>
> The difference between killing one's self and bringing one's life to a responsible good end is the very difference between pathological and rational suicide. ... (Etkind, 1997, p. 107).

XIV. Conclusion: What Do Nearly All Suicides Have in Common?

Dying is the one thing - perhaps the only thing - in life you don't have to do. Stick around long enough and it will be done for you.
                                                                    - Edwin Shneidman

It is appropriate that Edwin Shneidman, who is referred to numerous times in this book, provides its conclusion. He was the founding President of the American Association of Suicidology and first chief of the Center for the Study of Suicide Prevention at the National Institute of Mental Health. In 1975 he became the first Professor of Thanatology at the University of California at Los Angeles. With Dr. Norbert Farberow he pioneered the training of nonprofessionals for telephone crisis intervention. They also accomplished a landmark study of suicide notes as part of an effort to understand and prevent suicide. His first book, *Deaths of Man* (1973) was nominated for the National Book Award in Science. A later book, *The Suicidal Mind* (1996), brims with insight into the suicidal impulse and how it can be counteracted. His last book, *A Commonsense Book of Death: Reflections at Ninety of a Lifelong Thanatologist* (2008), is a thoughtful culmination to his distinguished career.

After nearly a half-century of studying suicide Shneidman offered this observation:

> ... all the committed suicidal people I have studied over the years, independent of their different psychological needs - exhibited a certain set of psychological characteristics. In the cauldron of thought, I have boiled these down to ten commonalities of suicide.
>
> By "commonality" I mean a feature that is present in 95 out of 100 committed suicides - an aspect of thought, feeling, or behavior that occurs in almost every case of suicide. (1996, pp. 129-130).

XIV.   Conclusion: What Do Nearly All Suicides Have in Common?

The balance of this chapter presents these ten commonalities with commentary.

1. The common purpose of suicide is to seek a solution (p. 131).

There is a purpose to every suicide. "To understand what a suicide is about, we must understand the psychological problem the suicidal person intends to address" (p. 130). Robert Dwyer (chapter IV and XIII) and Brett Wallace (chapter V) were facing prison sentences. Both determined suicide would solve the problems of incarceration and humiliation. Thomas Youk, a 53 year-old man waiting to die from Amyotrophic Lateral Sclerosis, reached out to Dr. Jack Kevorkian with a request to be euthanized. (Such a request is a self-determined death.) In the movie, "A Few Good Men," a disillusioned Marine officer, Lt. Col. Matthew Markinson, commits suicide when faced with the dilemma of either betraying his commanding officer or allowing two innocent soldiers to go to prison.

2. The common goal of suicide is to seek a cessation of consciousness (p. 131).

In the Hebrew Bible the suffering Job cries out to God, "When I think my bed will comfort me and my couch will ease my complaint, even then you frighten me with dreams and terrify me with visions, so that I prefer strangling than this body of mine" (Job 7:13-14, NIV).
In Pat Conroy's novel, *The Prince of Tides*, the suicidal character Savannah Wingo is tormented by the memory of a her childhood rape. Conroy described her anguish with these words: "Rape is a crime against sleep and memory; its afterimage imprints itself like an irreversible negative from the camera obscura of dreams" (2017). Job and Savannah wanted an end to consciousness. Job is unable to find it in sleep; Savannah seeks it by attempting suicide.

3. The common stimulus of suicide is unbearable psychological pain (p. 131).

Arguably there is no greater emotional pain than that of a parent who has lost of a child. The writer Anne Rice knows this pain, having lost her five-year-old daughter to leukemia. Fearing she would continue on a downward spiral into alcoholism and eventually commit suicide, Anne returned to writing, taking an unpublished short story and expanding it into the bestselling novel *Interview with the Vampire* (1976).

Unfortunately, the story of Captain Charles McVay ended with his suicide. In World War II the heavy cruiser USS Indianapolis was hit by a torpedo. Three-hundred of the crew went down with the ship, leaving 896 men adrift in the Pacific Ocean. Tragically, 579 of the survivors were taken by sharks, leaving 317 to be rescued four days after the Indianapolis went down. Captain McVay was court martialed in 1945 and found guilty of mismanaging the ship. He was exonerated in 2000 following a United States Congress investigation, 32 years after his suicide by a self-inflicted gunshot. He was discovered on the front lawn of his home, holding a toy sailor in one hand. Possibly he would not have committed suicide had his exoneration come earlier. It is also possible that the ineffable psychological pain from losing so many of his men in such a ghastly manner was beyond palliation.

4. The common stressor in suicide is frustrated psychological needs (p. 131).

The renown psychologist Henry Murray's *Explorations in Personality* (1938) explains human behavior in terms of the need to satisfy one or more of 26 needs. The inference of his work is behavior always makes sense if it is considered as an attempt to satiate a need. In the movie, "The Mission," Rodrigo Mendoza, portrayed by Robert DiNero, seeks to satisfy his need for *abasement* (punishment for a misdeed) by starving himself to death. In a fit of rage Mendoza had killed his brother.

Murray included the needs to be seen and heard (*exhibitionism*) and influence others (*dominance*) in his list of psychogenic needs. A stunning example of suicide as a response to these needs is a Buddhist monk who commits suicide by immolation as a form of protest..

One of Shneidman's patients, Ariel Wilson, attempted suicide by immolation. She was motivated by a frustrated need for a life in which she would be supported, nurtured, protected, and loved. Murray referred to these needs as *succorance*. Ariel lived three years in unremitting pain as a burn patient before dying at age 22.

5. The common emotion in suicide is hopelessness/helplessness (p. 131).

It would be too much to ask anyone to imagine the hopelessness and helplessness of the 15 people who jumped to their death from the World Trade Center on 9/11/2001. Faced with imminent incineration they chose how they would die since death was inevitable. When a person is in despair and believes there is no possibility of help then suffering or suicide are the only alternatives.

6. The common cognitive state in suicide is ambivalence (p. 131).

The near suicides of Eric Hoffer and Augusten Burroughs, described in chapter VI, express ambivalence. Ultimately both wanted to live, but not live the life he had. And both came to the realization that his life could be ended without dying. For Hoffer it meant traveling from town to town: "I did not commit suicide," he wrote, "but on that Sunday a workingman died and a tramp was born" (1983, p. 25). For Burroughs it meant changing everything about his life that could be changed. "What did I really need to be reborn?" he wondered, "Maybe just two things. A door. And then a highway" (2012, p. 100). Kevin Hines, who survived a jump from the Golden Gate Bridge, realized on the way down that he didn't want to die. He is another example of someone who simultaneously wants to die and does not want to die.

Even some accomplished suicides show evidence of ambivalence. *Hesitation wounds* result from a reluctance to complete the act. It is not unusual to see two or three superficial cuts on a wrist in addition to the final and fatal incision. Neither is it unusual for an accomplished suicide to be preceded by an apparent intention to live. For instance, the college student who registers for classes, purchases textbooks, and then commits suicide.

7. The common perceptual state of suicide is constriction (p. 131).

Constricted thinking does not allow thoughts that might abort a suicide attempt. The past and future are shrouded by the painful present. "A person who commits suicide turns off all ties to the past, declares a kind of mental bankruptcy, and his or her memories have no lien" (p. 134). The temporary seems permanent and the adage, "This too shall come to pass" does not come to mind. In addition, reaching out for help is considered futile. Mary Karr recognized this and in her poem, "Incant Against Suicide," she admonishes, "Your head's a bad neighborhood, don't go there alone, even if you have to stop strangers to ask the way" (2001, p. 3).

8. The common action in suicide is escape or egression (p. 131).

The tragedy of the aforementioned 9/11 suicides is a rare and dramatic instance of a compelling need to escape. The mass suicide at Masada (chapter II) was driven by the need to escape capture by the Romans and enslavement. Both are exceptional instances of suicide for the purpose of escaping a situation. Much more often, the need to exit is far less convincing to those left behind:

> Suicide is the ultimate egression, besides which running away from home, quitting a job, deserting an army, or leaving a spouse - all egressions or escapes -pale in comparison. We speak of "unplugging the world" when we go on vacation or bury ourselves in a good book, but most of us distinguish between the wish to get away for a while and the desire to shut out life forever (p. 134).

9. The common interpersonal act in suicide is communication of intention (p. 131).

Concerning psychological autopsies, Shneidman wrote, "One of the most interesting things we found ... was that there were clues to the impending lethal event in the vast majority of cases" (p. 135). In his memoir, *Darkness Visible*, William Styron describes responding to a perfunctory greeting from a perfect stranger with, "I'm dying" (1992). Certainly this was a melancholic disclosure, but is it reasonable to have expected the stranger to recognize Styron's response as a communication of suicidal intention? Jesus said, "He that hath ears to hear, let him hear" (Matthew 11:15, KJV). Do the untrained have ears to hear when a suicide is imminent? Shneidman thinks not when the verbal and behavioral communications are discreet. But they are often indiscreet and "audible if one has ears and wits to hear them" (1996, p. 135). Moreover, suicide itself can be an attempt at communication when all other forms of communication have failed.

10. The common pattern in suicide is consistent with lifelong styles of coping (p. 131).

A psychiatrist, Lewis Wolberg, conducted an ingenious experiment in which he demonstrated how people resolve conflict situations in a manner that is consistent with their lifelong coping mechanisms (1972, pp. 10-12). "People are enormously loyal to themselves, and they show this by the consistency of their reactions to certain aspects of life throughout its span" (Shneidman, 1996, p. 135). Of course, suicide is a maladaptive coping mechanism that can be resorted to only once. However, as Shnediman pointed out, "(The) repetition of a tendency to capitulate, to flee, to blot it out, to escape is perhaps the most telling single clue to an ultimate suicide" (p. 136).

Glossary

Absorb: A principle of preventing a suicide attempt in progress in which the intervener must be prepared to hear misdirected anger and accusations from the suicidal person and not respond with anger or defensiveness.

Accomplished Suicide: An alternative term for "successful suicide," which has an oxymoronic implication.

Altruistic Suicide: One of Emil Durkheim's four categories of suicide in which an individual willingly dies for another or others.

Ambivalence: A characteristic of many accomplished suicides and suicide attempts in which the person expressed simultaneous and contradictory feelings of wanting to die and not wanting to die.

Anomic Suicide: One of Emil Durkheim's four categories of suicide in which an individual cannot adjust to social change and has lost his or her accustomed relationships and/or standing in society.

Antinatalism: The moral position currently associated with philosopher David Benatar that having children is immoral because they have no choice regarding their existence and the painfulness of life.

Annihilation: The afterlife belief that there is no existence after death.

Anorexia Nervosa: An eating disorder characterized by unhealthy weight loss, dysmorphia, and an obsession with low bodyweight.

Assessment Progression: Determining an individual's suicidality in four stages: (1) merely thinking about death (musing), (2) knowledge of the means for suicide, (3) possession of the means or a plan for acquisition, (4) determination of the time and place for the suicide.

Autoerotic Asphyxia: Also known as the "choking game" in which masturbation is accompanied by a scarf or other type of noose tied tightly around the neck so as to intensify an orgasm. Death will occur accidentally if the individual loses consciousness and it might appear as a suicide.

Cluster Suicides: Usually associated with teenage suicides, it is the phenomenon of one suicide triggering other suicides in the same locale.

Clues: Indications or hints from suicidal people that their suicide is imminent.

Comparative Bad: In philosophy, one of three criteria for something being bad or undesirable. Something is comparatively bad if it prevents something that would have been good or better. For instance, death is bad because it ends life and the pleasures that might have been.

Constriction: Depressed and suicidal individuals tend to isolate and limit their thinking in terms of how they view and evaluate their circumstances as well as options for changing their situations.

Crisis Intervention: One of three categories of suicide counseling (prevention and postvention are the other two). Crisis intervention is the counseling that occurs when a suicide attempt is in progress.

Defuse: A principle of preventing a suicide attempt in progress in which the guiding concept is each moment the suicide is delayed the less likely it will occur.

Deprivation Theory: Virtually synonymous with the concept of "comparative bad," this is the concept that something can be considered bad if it eliminates the possibility of something good. According to this theory, death is bad because it eliminates the possibility of the good things that life has to offer.

Deontological: An approach to moral philosophy by which moral rightness is determined according to principles all human beings are duty-bound to follow. It is in contrast to determining moral rightness according to a desired goal, expediency or comfort.

Egoistic Suicide: One of Emil Durkhiem's categories of suicide in which the suicide is result of alienation from the community. It characterizes those suicides that occur owing to the perception of being alone in the world.

Epidemiology: The statistical occurrence of a disease or health condition as part of an effort to address its cause and treatment.

Etiology: The study of the origin of a disease or condition as part of an effort to address its cause and treatment.

External Locus of Control: The tendency of an individual to believe significant conditions of his or her life are determined by other people. This tendency is frequently observed among adolescents and contributes to their depression.

Fatalistic Suicide: One of Emil Durkheim's four classifications of suicide in which an individual arrives at a determination of hopelessness and helplessness and opts for suicide.

Framing: An informal psychotherapeutic term for an individual's description and explanation for his or her circumstances. It is a description and explanation that might not be accurate and warrants challenging lest suicide becomes an option.

Global Thinking: A form of overgeneralizing in which the thoughts of an individual are characterized as the thoughts of "everybody" and/or a failure in a specific task is characterized as evidence of not being able to do "anything" right. Examples of global thinking are the statements "Everybody hates me" and "I can't do anything right, I'm a total loser." Such thinking is common among adolescents, but not restricted to them.

Hesitation Wounds: In accomplished suicides injuries that indicate or demonstrate ambivalence on the part of the deceased. For example, self-administered surface cuts on the wrist before the fatal incision is made.

Immediate and Total Thinking: A characteristic of child and adolescent thinking in which there is an unrealistic insistence on a complete resolution to a problem without delay.

Instrumental Bad: In philosophy, one of three criteria for something being bad or undesirable. Something is instrumentally bad if it is an agent that leads to something bad. Something that is instrumentally bad is not bad in and of itself.

Intrinsic Bad: In philosophy, one of three criteria for something being bad or undesirable. Something is intrinsically bad if it is bad in and of itself.

Lewy Body Dimentia: A neurological disorder characterized by compromised attention and alertness, recurrent visual hallucinations, dementia, and Parkinson's Disease symptoms. (LBD is sometimes misdiagnosed as Parkinson's Disease or Alzheimer's Disease.)

Negotiate: A principle of crisis intervention in which the suicidal individual is encouraged to delay the act. The appeal must be realistic. For example, the individual is asked to wait for a mental health professional or significant person to arrive for a conversation.

Nondisclosure: The stipulation in a life insurance policy in which the insurance company will not pay the benefit to beneficiaries if the deceased failed to disclose a medical or psychological condition.

Ockham's Razor: Also known as the *principle of parsimony*, it teaches that explanations should be as uncomplicated as possible. Its

Latin expression is, *Entia non sunt multiplicanda praeter necessitatem*. Translated into English, it reads, "Entities should not be multiplied beyond necessity."

Permanent Thinking: A characteristic of child and adolescent thinking in which temporary conditions are seen as unchangeable and solvable problems as unsolvable.

Postvention: The provision of care and comfort to those who have lost a relative, friend or other associate to suicide.

Prevention: Any effort to address suicide before an attempt is made. The effort can be directed toward an individual's suicidality or suicide as a community or national problem.

Psychache: The term coined by Edwin Shneidman to refer to unbearable psychological-emotional pain.

Psychogenic Needs: Identified by psychologist Henry Murray, the 26 emotional necessities that motivate human behavior.

Psychological Autopsies: The investigative method developed by Edwin Shneidman and Norman Farberow to determine if a death was a suicide and, if a suicide, what motivated it.

Rational Suicide: A self-determined death that was well-reasoned and arguably justifiable in contrast to one that resulted from unsoundness of mind.

Reframe: A psychotherapeutic term associated with Cognitive Behavioral Therapy in which individuals are challenged to explain and describe their circumstances more optimistically. These alternative explanations and descriptions must be reasonable and realistic.

Remain: A principle of crisis intervention in which the imminently suicidal person is not left alone. The intervener stays with the individual as long as staying will not result in the intervener's injury or death.

Self-Mutilation: Colloquially referred to as "cutting," it is a coping mechanism in which physical self-injury is used to alleviate distress or emotional pain.

Suicide: (1) A death that was self-determined and self-administered. (2) An individual who has accomplished a self-determined, self-administered death.

Suicidology: The formal study of self-determined, self-administered deaths.

Suicide Myths: Widely held incorrect beliefs and misperceptions concerning suicide.

Suicide Survivors: Individuals who have lost a relative, friend or other associate to suicide.

Teleological: An approach to moral philosophy by which moral rightness is determined according to a desired goal, expediency or comfort. It is in contrast to determining moral rightness according to principles all human beings are duty-bound to follow.

Thanatology: The formal study of death, dying, and bereavement.

References

Introduction

Camus, A. *The myth of Sisyphus and other essays*. New York: Alfred A. Knopf, Inc.

Evans, G. and Farberow, N. (1988). *The encyclopedia of suicide*. New York: Facts on File.

Jamison, K.R. (2000). *Night falls fast: Understanding suicide*. New York: Alfred A. Knopf.

Joiner, T. (2010). *Myths about suicide*. Cambridge, MA: Harvard University Press.

Kant, I. Recovered from Quoteland.com on November 23, 2016.

Schneider-Williams, S. (10/27/2016). "The terrorist inside my husband's brain." *Neurology*. 87 (13): 1308-1311.

Stanford Encyclopedia of Philosophy (05/18/2004). "Suicide." Palo Alto, CA: Stanford University.

I. Epidemiology

Evans, G. and Farberow, N. (1988). *The encyclopedia of suicide*. New York: Facts on File.

Parker-Pope, T. (05/02/2013). "Suicide rates rise sharply in U.S." *New York Times*.

Paulos, J. (1995). *A mathematician reads the newspaper*. New York: Basic Books.

II. Etiology

Adler, A. (2016). Recovered from greatquotes.com website on 12/12/2016.

Bacon, F. (2016). Recovered from www.azquotes.com website on 12/04/2016.

Burns, O. (1984). *Cold sassy tree*. New York: Houghton Mifflin Company.

Camus, A. (1955). *The myth of Sisyphus and other essays*: New York: Random House.

Daily Mail. (2014). "Designer L'Wren Scott was 'embarrassed and millions in debt' when she committed suicide in her Manhattan apartment while 'devastated' lover Mick Jagger was on tour   in Australia." 03/17/2014.

Durkheim, E. (1897). *Le suicide: Etudie de sociologie*. Paris, France: Alcan.

Evans, G. and Farberow, N. (1988). *The encyclopedia of suicide*. New York: Facts on File.

Frankl, V. (1959). *Man's search for meaning*. New York: Washington Square Press.

Freud, S. (1933). "Mourning and melancholia." *Collected papers*, volume II . London: Hogarth Press.

Gernsbacher, L. (1988). *The suicide syndrome: Origins, manifestations, and alleviation of human self-destructiveness*. New York: Human Sciences Press, Inc.

Grollman, E. (1988). *Suicide: Prevention, intervention, postvention*. Boston, MA: Beacon Press.

Hugo, V. (1987). *Les miserables.* translated by Fahnestock, L. & McAfee, N. New York: Signet Classics.

James, W. (1902). *The varieties of religious experience: A study in human nature.* New York: Random House.

Jamison, K. (1995). *An unquiet mind.* New York: Random House.

Joiner, T. (2010). *Myths about suicide.* Cambridge, MA; Harvard University Press.

King, S. (1982). *Rita Hayworth and shawshank redmption: Different seasons.* New York: Viking Press. Penguin Group.

Kretzmer, H. (1986). "Javert's suicide song." (English lyrics). "Les Miserables." New York: Broadway Production.

Kubler-Ross, E. (1969). *On death and dying.* New York: Macmillan.

Lester, D. (2005). *Suicide in the holocaust.* Hauppauge, NY: Nova Science Publishers.

Malikow, M. (2014). *Profiles in character: Twenty-six stories that will instruct and inspire teenagers.* Lanham, MD: University Press of America.

Menninger, K. (1938). *Man against himself.* New York: Harcourt, Brace and World, Inc.

Murphy-O'Connor, J. and Cunliffe, B. (2008). *The holy land: Oxford archaeological guides (5th ed.).* Oxford, UK: Oxford University Press.

Poe, E. (2014). *"The black cat." Restored Publication Writing Services.* Charleston, SC: Createspace Publishing.

Shneidman, E. (2004). *Deaths of man.* New York: Jason Aronson Publishers.

Spenser, E. (2016). *Recovered from http://www.brainyquote.com on 12/12/2016.*

Styron, W. (1990). *Darkness visible: A memoir of madness.* New York: Random House.

Tolstoy, L. (1929). *My confession, my religion, the gospel in brief.* New York: Charles Scribner.

Von Andics, M. (1947). *Suicide and the meaning of life.* London: William Hodge.

III. Suicide and Resilience

Aristotle. (1999). *Nichomachean ethics.* Book VIII, 119. Indianapolis, IN: Hackett.

Armstrong, L. with Jenkins, S. (2000). *It's not about the bike: My journey back to life.* New York: Berkely Books.

Brown, H.J. (2012). www.motivatingquotes.com/perseverance. htm. Recovered 06/18/2012.

Camus, A. (2011). Quote recovered from Motivational Memo website on January 1, 2011.

Charney, D. (2010). "This emotional life." PBS telecast, January 2010. Kunhardt McGee Production.

Cohen, R. (2004). *Blinsided: A reluctant memoir – living a life above illness.* New York: Harper Collins Publishers.

Coles, R. (1998). *The moral intelligence of children: How to raise a moral child.* New York: Random House.

Culver, J. (1989). "A deadly struggle against the sea." *People.* 08/21/1989.

Deford, F. (1981). "Kenny, dying young." *Sports Illustrated*. 03/09/1981.

Frankl, V. (1959). *Man's search for meaning*. New York: Washington Square Press.

Jamison, K. (1996). *Touched with fire: Manic depressive illness and the artistic temperment*. New York: Simon and Schuster: Free Press

Kelly, N. (2012). Unpublished interview conducted 06/16/2012.

Kilpatrick, W. (1992). *Why Johnny can't tell right from wrong: Moral illiteracy and the case for character education*. New York: Simon and Schuster.

Kipling, R. (1910). "If." *Rewards and Fairies*. Garden City, NY: Doubleday Page & Compnay.

Kushner, H. (2002). *Living a life that matters*. New York: Alfred A. Knopf. Random House.

Malikow, M. (2008). *Profiles in character: Twenty-six stories that will instruct and inspire teenagers*. Lanham, MD: University Press of America.

_____. (2009) *Suicidal thoughts: Essays on self-determined death*. Lanham, MD: Hamilton Books.

_____. (2010). *Being human: Philosophical reflections on psychological issues*. Lanham, MD: Hamilton Books.

Maltsberger, J. (1987). Keynote address at the annual meeting of the American Association of Suicidologists. Boston, MA.

Myers, D. (2007). *Psychology: Eighth Edition*. New York: Worth Publishers.

Shneidman, E. (1998). *The suicidal mind.* New York: Oxford University Press.

Shenk, J. (2005). "Lincoln's great depression." *The Atlantic Monthly.* October 2005.

Shumaker, B. (2010). "This emotional life." PBS telecast, January 2010. Kunhardt McGee Production.

Stingley, D. (1983). *Happy to be alive.* New York: Beaufort Books.

Swofford, A. (2012). "We pretend the vets don't even exist." *Newsweek.* 05/28/2012.

Trelease, J. (1985). *I read aloud because my father read to me: The new read aloud handbook.* New York: Penguin Books.

Wicker, C. (1989). "The man sentenced to life." Orlando Sentinel. 05/29/1989.

IV. Suicide Myths

Amery, J. (1999). *On suicide: A discourse on voluntary death.* Bloomington, IN: Indiana University Press.

Braak, Y. (2007). "The aging of holocaust survivors: Myth and reality." *Israeli Medical Association Journal.* Volume 9. March, 2007.

Caruso, K. (2016). "Suicide myths." Recovered from Suicide.org website on 12/21/2016).

Chang, B; Gitlin, D; Patel, R (2011). "The depressed patient and suicidal patient in the emergency department: evidence-based management and treatment strategies". Emergency medicine practice. 13 (9): 1–23.

Hoffer, E. (1983). *Truth imagined.* Titusville, NJ: Hopewell Publications, LLC.

Joiner, T. (2010). *Myths about suicide.* Cambridge, MA: Harvard University Press.

Klagsbrun, F. (1976). *Too young to die: Youth and suicide.* New York: Houghton-Mifflin.

Lester, D. (1999). *Making sense of suicide: An in-depth look at why people kill themselves.* Philadelphia, PA: The Charles press, Publishers, Inc.

Malikow, M. (2009). *Suicidal thoughts: Essays on self-determined death.* Lanham, MD: Hamilton Books.

Medical Record. (1901). "A man named Edgar J. Briggs." 60(1901): 660-661.

New York Times (2017). "Suicide and suicidal behavior." Health Guide. 01/06/2017.

Nuland, S. (1993). *How we die: reflections on life's final chapter.* New York: Alfred A. Knopf, Inc.

Redfield-Jamison, K. (1999). *Night falls fast: Understanding suicide.* New York: Alfred A. Knopf, Inc.

Rosin, H. (2015). "The silicon valley suicides." *The Atlantic.* December, 2015.

Selden, R. (1978). "Where are they now: A follow up study of suicide-attempters from the Golden Gate Bridge." *Suicide and life threatening behavior*, 8, 1-13.

"The Bridge." (2007). Port Washington, NY: KOCH Lorber Films.

References

Tintinalli, J. (2010). *Emergency medicine: A comprehensive study guide.* New York: McGraw-Hill Companies.

Traubmann, T. (2005). "Study: Holocaust survivors 3 times more likely to attempt suicide." Haaretz. www.haaretz.com/news/study - holocaust - survivors. 08/10/2005.

Wiesel, E. (1987). "Con l'incubo che tutto sia accaduto invano." *La Stampa,* Turin, 04/14/1987.

V. Suicide Prevention

Collins, J. (2003). *Sanity and grace: A journey of suicide, survival, and strength.* New York: Penguin Group.

Grollman, E. and Malikow, M. (1999). *Living when a young friend commits suicide: Or even starts talking about it.* Boston, MA: Beacon Press.

Lester, D. (1997). *Making sense of suicide: An in-depth loo at why people kill themselves.* Philadelphia, PA: The Charles Press, Publishers.

Shneidman, E. (1996). *The suicidal mind.* New York: Oxford University Press.

Viorst, J. (1986). *Necessary losses: The loves, illusions, dependencies, and impossible expectations that all of us have to give up in order to grow.* New York: Simon and Schuster.

VI. Crisis Intervention

Burroughs, A. (2012). *This is how: Help for overcoming the self.* New York: St. Martin's Press.

Donne, J. (1624). *Devotions upon emergent occasions: Meditation 17.* Recovered from PoemHunter.com on 01/03/2017.

Heckler, R. (1994). *Waking up alive: The descent, the suicide attempt & return to life*. New York: G.P. Putnam's Sons.

Hoffer, E. (1983). *Truth imagined*. New York: Harper & Row, Publishers.

Livingston, G. (2004). *Too soon old, too late smart: Thirty true things you need to know*. New York: Marlowe & Company.

Malikow, M. (1991). *The preparedness of evangelical pastors for the provision of suicide postvention counseling* (unpublished doctoral dissertation). Boston, MA: Boston University.

Percy, W. (1983). *Lost in the cosmos: The last self help book*. New York: Picador.

Shneidman, E. (1998). *The suicidal mind*. New York: Oxford University Press.

VII. Suicide Postvention

Livingston, G. (2004). *Too soon old, too late smart: Thirty true things you need to know*. New York: Marlowe & Company.

Malikow, M. (1991). *The preparedness of evangleical pastors for the provision of suicide postvention counseling.* (unpublished doctoral dissertation.) Boston, MA: Boston University.

Shneidman, E. (1972). Survivors of suicide. Cain, A, editor. Springfield, IL: Charles C. Thomas.

Smith, J. (1986). *Coping with suicide*. New York: The Rosen Publishing Group, Inc.

VIII. Depression and Suicide

Antony, M. and Swinson, R. (2009). *When being perfect isn't good enough: Strategies for coping with perfectionism*. Oakland, CA: New Harbinger Publications.

Camus, A. (1955). *The myth of Sisyphus and other essays*. New York: Alfred K. Knopf, Inc.

_____. (1991). *The myth of Sisyphus and other essays*. New York: Vintage Books.

Cowper, W. (2017). "Hatred and vengeance: My eternal portion. (Lines written during a period of insanity)." Recovered from http://www.poetryfoundation.org/poems&poets/detail/50600 on 05/11/2017.

Eliot, T. (2017). "The love song of J. Alfred Prufrock." Recovered from the Poetry Foundation website on January 30, 2017.

Gernsbacher, L. (1988). *The suicide syndrome: Origins, manifestations, and alleviation of human self-destructiveness*. New York: Human Sciences Press, Inc.

Goleman, D. (1996). "Higher suicide risk for perfectionists." *The New York Times*. May 1, 1996.

Halgin, R. and Whitbourne, K. (2000). *Abnormal psychology: Clinical perspectives on psychological disorders, third edition*. New York: McGraw - Hill Higher Education.

Hotchner, A.E. (2005). *Papa Hemingway: A personal memoir*. Cambridge, MA: De Capo Press Perseus Books.

Jung, C. (1933). *Modern man in search of a soul*. New York: Harcourt, Brace, Jovanovich, Publishers.

Kessler, R., McGonagle, K., Zao, S., Nelson, C., Hughes, M., Eshleman, S., Witchen, H., and Kendler, K. (1994). "lifetime and 12-month prevalence of DSM III-R psychiatric patients in the

United States." National comorbidity survey. *Archives of general psychiatry*, 51, 8-19.

Levingston, S. (2014). "The high suicide rate among elderly white men, who may suffer from depression." *The Washington Post*. December 8, 2014.

Malikow, M. (2007). *Profiles in character: Twenty-six stories that will instruct and inspire teenagers*. Lanham, MD: University Press of America.

Maltsberger, J. (1987). Keynote address presented at the annual meeting of the American Association of Suicidology. Boston, MA.

May, R. (1969). *Love and will*. New York: Norton.

McCullough, C. (1979). *The thornbirds*. New York: Avon Books.

Nouwen, H. (1999). *The inner voice of love: A journey through anguish to freedom*. Los Angeles, CA: Image Books, Inc.

Plath, S. (1971). *The bell jar*. New York: Harper & Row.

Redfield-Jamison, K. (1993). *Touched with fire: Manic-depressive illness and the artistic temperament*. New York: The Free Press.

Shenk, J. (2005). "Lincoln's great depression." *The Atlantic monthly*. October 2005.

Styron, W. (1992). *Darkness visible: A memoir of madness*. New York: Vintage Books.

Wallace, D.F. (1998). "The depressed person." *Harper's Magazine*. January, 1998.

_____ (2009). *This is water: Some thoughts delivered on a significant occasion, about living a compassionate life*. New York: Little, Brown, and Company.

IX. Adolescent Suicide

Berscheid, E. and Hatfield, E. (1969). *Interpersonal attraction*. New York: Addison-Wesley.

Burroughs, A. (2012). *This is how: Help for the self*. New York: St. Martin's Press.

Chance, S. (1992). *Stronger than death: When suicide touches your life*. New York: W.W. Norton & Co.

Dickens, C. (1999). *A tale of two cities*. New York: Dover Thrift Editions.

Dobson, J. (1978). *Preparing for adolescence*. Santa Ana, CA: Vision House.

Ian, J. (1975). "At seventeen." New York: Columbia Records.

Redfield-Jamison, K. (1999). *Night falls fast: Understanding suicide*. New York: Alfred A. Knopf.

Rosin, H. (2015). "Why are so many kids killing themselves in Palo Alto?" *The Atlantic*. December, 2015.

"World's greatest dad." (2009). Los Angeles, CA: Darko Entertainment.

X. Altruistic and Rational Suicides

Burroughs, A. (2012). *This is how: Help for the* self. New York: St. Martin's Press.

Churchill, W. (2017). Recovered from https://www.brainyquote. com on 02/19/2017.

King, M. (2017). Recovered from https://brainyquote.com on 02/19/2017.

Hoffer, E. (1983). *Truth imagined*. New York: Harper & Row, Publishers.

Lincoln, A. (2017). Recovered from https://www.american-rhetoric.com/speeches/gettysburg on 02/19/2017.

Nuland, S. (1995). *How we die: Reflections on life's final chapter*. New York: Random House.

XI. Suicide as an Ethical Issue

Blackstone. W. 1765-69. *Commentaries on the laws of England. Book IV*.

Grollman, E. 1988. *Suicide: Prevention, intervention, postvention*. Boston: Beacon Press.

Holdsworth, W.S. 1926. *History of English law*. London: Methuen.

Maltsberger, J. (1987). Annual Conference of the American Association of Suicidologists. Sponsor: Harvard School of Medicine. Boston, MA: Copley Plaza Hotel.

Nuland, S. 1995. *How we die*. New York: Random House.

Plato. *Phaedo*. translated: Tredennick, H. New York: Penguin Books. 1962.

Shneidman, E. "Suicide as Psychache." Journal of Nervous and Mental Disease.Vol. 181. No. 3. March, 1993.

_____. 1996. *The suicidal mind.* New York: Oxford University Press.

Smith Kennedy, J. and Plimpton, G. 1993. *Chronicles of courage: Very special artists.* New York: Random House.

XII. Thanatology

Benetar, D. (2006). *Better never to have been: The harm of coming into existence.* Oxford, UK: Oxford University Press.

Epicurus. Recovered from http://www.brainyquote. com/ quotes/quotes/e/epicurus on 05/11/2016.

Kagan, S. (2012). *Death: What should we believe about the nature of death? How should the knowledge of our mortality affect the way we live?* New Haven, CT: Yale University Press.

Malikow, M. (2014). *Mere existentialism: A primer.* Chipley, FL: Theocentric Publishing Group.

Nagel, T. (1979). *Mortal questions.* New York: Cambridge University Press.

Neider, C. (Editor). (1990). *The autobiography of Mark Twain.* New York: Perennial.

Plato. (399 B.C.E.) *Apology.* Translated by Benjamin Jowett. Recovered from the Internet Classic Archive on 05/12/2016.

Preston, B. and Fisher, B. (1974). "Nothing from Nothing." Santa Monica, CA: A & M Recording.

"The Unforgiven." (1992). Burbank, CA: Warner Brothers.

Whittier, J.G. (1856). "Maude Muller." Recovered from Bartelby.com website on 05/19/2016.

XIII. Suicide Notes

Breitbart, W. and Rosenfeld, B. (2011). "Physician assisted suicide: The influence of psychosocial issues." Tampa, FL: Moffitt Cancer Center. 02/27/2011.

Brinkley, D. (2008). *"Football season is over Dr. Hunter S. Thompson's final note ... Entering the no more fun zone."* Rolling Stone. June 19, 2008.

Cobain, K. (2017). Recovered from http://www.rotten.com /library/death/suicide-notes/ on 04/07/2017.

Etkind, M. (1997). *Or not to be: A collection of suicide notes.* New York: The Berkley Publishing Group.

Evans, G. and Farberow, N. (1988). *The encyclopedia of suicide.* New York: Facts on File.

Hitler, A. (2017). Recovered from http://www.auschwitz.dk/ Will.htm on 03/31/2017.

Kellner, B. (1991). *The last dandy: Ralph Barton.* Columbia, MO: University of Missouri Press.

Lindsay, D. "George Eastman: The final shot." *American Experience.* PBS. Retrieved 08/30/2013.

Malikow, M. (2016). *It happened in Little Valley: A case study of uxoricide.* Chipley, FL: Theocentric Publishing Company.

Maris, R., Berman, A., and Silverman, M. (2000). *Comprehensive textbook of suicidology.* New York: The Guilford Press.

Montgomery, L. (2008). "Is this Lucy Maud's suicide note?". The Globe and Mail. September 25, 2008. Retriever 04/12/2017.

Muha, L. (1988). "Witnesses to tragedy." Long Island, NY: Newsday. January 21, 1988.

Nuland, S. (1995). *How we die: reflections on life's final chapter.* New York: Vintage Books.

Prinze, F. (2017). Recovered from http://www.rotten.com/ library/death/suicide-notes/ on 04/07/2017.

Redfield-Jamison, K. (1999). *Night falls fast: Understanding suicide.* New York: Alfred A. Knopf.

Sanders, G. (2017). Recovered from http://classicmoviechat. com/george-sanders-bored-to-death/ on 04/11/2017.

Shneidman, E. S. & Farberow, N. L. (1957). "Some comparisons between genuine and simulated suicide notes." *Journal of General Psychology*, 56, 251-256.

Schwarz, A. (2011). " A suicide, a last request, and a family's questions." *The New York Times*. 02/22/2011.

Stuart, C. (1993). "Report: Suicide note contained no confession." *Nashua Telegraph*. Associated Press. 02/01/1993 recovered on 04/12/2017.

Teasdale, S. (1933). "I Shall Not Care." *Rivers to the sea.* New York: The MacMillan Company.

Woolf, V. (2017). Recovered from www.openculture.com/ 2013/08/virginia - woolf - handwritten - suicide - note.html on 04/13/2017.

XIV. Conclusion

Burroughs, A. (2012). *This is how: Help for the self.* New York: St. Martin's Press.

Conroy, P. (2017). Recovered from http://goodreads.com/quotes. on 03/05/2017.

Hofffer, E. (1984). *Truth imagined*. New York: Harper and Row, Publishers.

Karr, M. (2001). *Viper rum*. New York: Penguin Poetry.

Murray, H. (1938). *Explorations in personality*. New York: Oxford University Press.

Rice, A. (1976). *Interview with the vampire*. New York: Alfred A. Knopf.

Shneidman, E. S. & Farberow, N. L. (1957). Some comparisons between genuine and simulated suicide notes. *Journal of General Psychology*, 56, 251-256.

Shneidman, E. (1973). *Deaths of man*. New York: Penguin Books.

_____. (1996). *The suicidal mind*. New York: Oxford University Press.

_____. (2008). *A commonsense book of death: Reflections at ninety of a lifelong thanatologist.*   Lanham, MD: Rowman and Littlefield.

Styron, W. (1990). *Darkness visible: A memoir of madness*. New York: Vintage Books.

Wolberg, L. (1972). *Hypnosis: Is it for you?* New York: Harcourt, Brace, Jovanovich, Inc.

About the Author

Max Malikow is on the faculty of the Renee Crown Honors Program of Syracuse University and an Adjunct Assistant Professor of Philosophy at LeMoyne College. He earned his Master's degree from Gordon-Conwell Theological Seminary and doctorate from Boston University. The author or editor of thirteen previous books, including three on suicide, he practices psychotherapy in Syracuse, New York.

www.ingramcontent.com/pod-product-compliance
Lightning Source LLC
Chambersburg PA
CBHW072252270326
41930CB00010B/2355